Did I Hear You Write?

Did I Hear You Write?

Michael Rosen

Five Leaves

Did I Hear You Write?

Second edition published in 1998
by Five Leaves Publications,
PO Box 81, Nottingham NG5 4ER

First published by André Deutch in 1989

0 907 123 76 7

Published with financial assistance from

EAST
MIDLANDS
ARTS

Printed in Great Britain by Antony Rowe
Design by 4 Sheets.

Cover photographs of Michael Rosen
at Barley Lane Primary School,
courtesy of *Ilford Recorder*

Contents

Acknowledgments

The first draft of this book was written while I was writer-in-residence at the Western Australian College of Advanced Education in Perth. I would like to thank Ken Willis, Eric Carlin and Bill Grono for getting me there and exposing me to the kinds of questions that prompted the writing of this book. I would like to thank Myra Barrs for reading the second draft and helping me scrap irrelevant and intemperate passages. Pam Royds, at André Deutsch was a superb editor, clarifying and improving a great deal. I would also like to thank the teachers who have invited me to their schools. This book would not have been written if I had not had those many opportunities. I would especially like to mention Jim Payne, Stephen Eyers, John Richmond and Helen Savva at Vauxhall Manor, Terry Staples at Holloway, Alex Moore at Brondesbury and Kilburn, Penny Bentley, Tracy Argent, Nik Chakraborty and Frank Tarrant at John Scurr. In rather obvious ways this would never have been written if it wasn't for Harold and Connie Rosen. I like to tell myself that Mum would have liked it, while Harold played a part between drafts two and three. Geraldine Clark Rosen said that I was like a bear with a sore head while I was writing the book. Make of that what you will but I should like to thank her here for hanging on in there in the bear-pit.

Introduction

Since 1976, as a result of my having written books for children, I've been working in and around schools. Sometimes this has meant that I have simply come to a school and done a performance, but at other times it has meant that I have got involved with helping children to write. There is nothing strange about this. As anyone reading this probably knows, many writers now spend time working with children — people like Jan Mark, John Agard, Judith Nicholls, Gillian Clarke, Adrian Mitchell, Lewis Nkosi, James Berry and many others. Each of us has to develop a way of working that makes sense for the children we meet, the teachers and ourselves. We make adjustments and compromises to fit the situation: what does the teacher expect? what kinds of writing and reading have the children done already? what kind of children are they? what have I just written that might interest them? These kinds of questions are asked in the context of the national institution called 'Education'. We find ourselves working right in the middle of the debate about 'standards', selection, streaming and testing, the National Curriculum and the morale and status of teachers.

More specifically, we also find ourselves in the middle of arguments about 'language'. None of us can be unaware of the noise about spelling, 'writing sentences', grammar and literacy — or, on the reading side — arguments about 'good literature' or 'English Literature'. In fact, for me, that is precisely what is exciting about going into schools and working with children. I feel that I am operating right in the eye of the storm, at the very point where all the experts and commentators, researchers and politicians cluster. There's me, there's some children, here's a book, there's a piece of paper and here's a pen. Now what?

And 'now what' is what this book is about, embedded in the questions and considerations raised by the contexts I find myself in: schools, children, teachers, the process of schooling.

II

When I read a book like this, I quite like to know 'where the writer's coming from'. Guessing that you feel the same way, I'll try and give you an idea of how I came to write this book.

My dad says that people sometimes come up to him and say, 'Are you Michael Rosen's dad?' But my experience is: 'Are you Harold and Connie Rosen's son?' When I say I am, they sometimes say, 'Oh well, that explains it.' This leaves me a bit confused, because I feel that the person is somehow saying that my being a writer of children's books was a foregone conclusion. I can't say it feels like that. After all, my brother was brought up by the same people and he's a geologist — well, a marine geologist, no I mean a marine ecologist — anyway, he doesn't write children's books. But then, maybe they are a bit right. Being Harold and Connie's son does explain a good deal.

When my friends came over to my house they used to stand in our front room and stare at all the books. All up the walls, across the mantelpiece, on the floor were books. 'Your dad hasn't read all these, has he?' they'd say. 'Yep, and my mum.' And then we'd get down to the important business. This meant going over to the massive reproduction of Breughel's 'Flemish Proverbs', on the sitting room wall, and finding all the rude bits. There was the man who was so uppity he thought he could piss on the moon, a big group of blokes all trying to get their bums into one toilet, couples kissing and heaven knows what.

Each in their own way, my parents showed me that books are storehouses. My mum read to me a lot when I was young, sitting on the edge of the bed reading me stories from all over the world. My dad took me to the local public library on Saturday mornings and vetted my choice of books with a quick 'You've read that once, haven't you?' or 'You're a bit old for that sort of stuff now, aren't you?' Every Christmas we got five of the latest bunch of Puffin books. Yet, though it sounds odd, I don't see myself as 'bookish' then. Though my dad would always ask 'Have you got a book on the go at the moment, Mick?', I spent hours and hours playing outside with my friend Harrybo, exploring the dirty stream that ran through our London suburb. I spent hours and hours locked in my bedroom with my brother while he talked his way through all his frustrations, angers, and pet hates. I spent hours and hours quizzing my mum at tea time about her childhood, about the war, about relatives. I spent hours and hours with my dad 'up the dump': a huge heap of rubbish and garbage that the local builder threw out each week. There was a wide circle of friends who came round or we visited and whole days were spent talking away about the state of the world, and the latest mad things that had happened — like trying to get the piano downstairs or how the shop below us managed to get us evicted.

As my parents were both teachers, they shared our holidays. We made for the countryside in England or France, with tents, primus stoves and rucksacks, camping far away from campsites, on farms by rivers and lakes and woods. Between the ages of five and twenty I must have spent in all about two years, camping, hiking, youth hostelling and the like.

Somehow or another my parents were able to manage a combination of being terribly bothered about me and at the same time give me an enormous amount of space. I wish I could have said the same about my schools.

Between the ages of three and eleven I went to ordinary state primary schools, that at that time were obsessed with the 'eleven-plus' selection exam, that decided whether you would go to a grammar school, (for brain-use) or a secondary modern, (for hand-use). This meant that

3

vast amounts of time were taken up with spelling tests, maths tests, English tests, intelligence tests, geography tests, history tests and even nature tests. At the age of ten, we were put in positions in class which changed each week according to how well or badly we had done in our tests. (The best position to be in was tenth, because then you were the bell monitor and had the job of walking up and down the corridor flinging an old brass bell about for twenty blissful seconds).

As the eleven-plus exam approached I became more and more jumpy and got the heeby-jeebies every night at bedtime. This was quite handy because it meant that Mum brought me up a cup of hot milk and brown sugar. She told me years later that there had been nothing to worry about anyway because the head master had told her that I had his 'recommendation' — (code for 'middle-class-boy-from-professional-home — we'll get him into a grammar school even if he fails the exam'.) I was quite cross when she told me that — the anxiety about the exam still hurt.

So I 'passed' and went to the co-ed grammar school that could never quite make up its mind whether it ought to be providing the services of a university kindergarten or a liberal arts college. So it was a strange mixture of rote learning, school plays, cross country running and detentions for not wearing school uniform. Every week for five years I had a 'composition' to do which would be a piece of writing entitled 'Rain' or 'Trees' or 'A day in the Sun'. Each week at home a little ritual would take place in and around this event.

Dad: Had any homework tonight?
Me: Yeah, a bit.
Dad: What was it?
Me: Nothing much.
Dad: What was it?
Me: English.
Dad: What did you have to do?
Me: No no, nothing much.

4

Dad: What did you have to do?

Me: A composition.

Dad: Let's have a look at it, then.

Me: No, it's OK. It's OK, it's in my bag.

Dad: Let's have a look at it.

(I get the composition.)

(He reads it.)

'Rain There are many kinds of rain...'

OR

'Trees There are many kinds of tree...'

Dad: Why have you written this?

Me: What do you mean?

Dad: You're not an expert on rain are you? You're not a meteorologist are you?

Me: No, I know, but it was what we were asked to do.

Dad: But you don't have to pretend you know about all kinds of rain. Just write about the rain you know.

Me: Uh?

Dad: The time you saw the rain coming across the hillside in Devon, the time you got rained on when you were cycling home from school... that sort of thing.

Me: Oh yeah...

And so each week, whatever the subject it went on for five years. Somewhere along the line, the message sunk in — *write about what you know.*

Academically, I was a success; I learnt how to pass exams and eventually, by way of thinking I was going to become a doctor(!), I ended up doing English Literature at Oxford University. This was a strange experience, as at that time English was regarded as a museum subject to study: it started hundreds of years before people spoke anything that looked or sounded like 'English' and ended before anyone around had been born. When I sat down to revise for that great marathon feat of writing, 'Finals', I looked down the list of names that represented 'English Literature': Chaucer, Skelton, Wyatt, Spenser, Shakespeare, Jonson, Milton, Dryden, Donne, Vaughan, Herbert, Congreve, Sheridan, Johnson, Defoe, Swift, Fielding, Wordsworth, Coleridge, Keats, Byron, Hardy, Hopkins, Clare. Before Chaucer I had 'Beowulf', Anglo-Saxon poetry and prose, a set of extracts from the eleventh to the fourteenth centuries and something called 'The Ballads'. As a body of human output it's quite a strange selection. It's not only a Germaine Greer who would notice that women don't seem to come in much, it's not only a Salman Rushdie who could notice that this selection of authors seems to imply that English men who write, live in a historic corridor inhabited only by fellow English men; and it doesn't take a Bertolt Brecht to notice that the selection excluded most oral and popular literature. In other words I studied the output of a group of middle and upperclass English men. (Exception: Clare). This wouldn't have mattered, if, at the outset, they had told us: 'Over the next three years you will study what a group of middle class English men have written over the last five hundred years.' But no, instead, we were constantly reminded that what this particular group of people had to say was the most important, the most universally appealing, the most insightful, the most inventive, the most significant literature available. I find it ironic that many of the 'greats' we studied like Shakespeare and Chaucer, immersed themselves in the folk and popular cultures of their own country and the literary cultures of the known world abroad. Whether they knew it or not they drew on the collective ingenuity and wisdom of Indians, Arabs, and peasants (see 'The Merchant's Tale' and 'The Taming of the Shrew'). Yet, our method of literary study proceeded chronologically as if English male writers begat English male writers down through the centuries. In a context like that, it is difficult to discover how the process of writing arises out of many cultural contexts: home, street, court, international, literate, non-literate, cosmopolitan, monocultural or whatever. Working as I do now, in the field of 'English Literature' (that is to say: I'm English and I write) I am frequently confronted by people who question me from the theoretical standpoint that accepts the main assumptions of an Oxford-type English Literature Course. Both the main argument of this book, and the implied argument of my writing does not accept those assumptions.

While I was at university I became very involved with theatre, and wrote, directed and acted in many plays. Occasionally I wrote what I thought were poems. These had a tendency to be densely metaphoric pieces addressed to a girlfriend somewhere. Somewhere in and around reading 'The Portrait of the Artist as a Young Man (James Joyce) and observing my mother putting together poetry magazine programmes for educational radio, I discovered another kind of writing: writing about my childhood in the voice of the child I once was. James Joyce had done it in prose narrative, e e cummings and Carl Sandburg seemed to be doing something similar in free verse, so why couldn't I? I was encouraged to write more and more of these pieces by my mother's producer at BBC Radio, Joan Griffiths, up to a point where I took my mother's job off her for a couple of years. Was she proud or resentful? I don't know.

Around 1972 I was bold enough to think I had enough to show to publishers, and Pam Royds, the children's editor at André Deutsch liked them enough to suggest that I be teamed up with the artist Quentin Blake to make 'Mind Your Own Business'.

III

'Mind Your Own Business' came at an interesting moment in that tiny world called 'Children's Poetry'. Schools and homes had their Robert Louis Stevenson's 'Child's Garden of Verses' and A.A. Milne's collections. They had their anthologies: 'A Book of a Thousand Poems' if they were 'fuddy-duddies', 'Voices' by Geoffrey Summerfield if they were 'moderns'. If they wanted to read writers writing at that very moment, in England, they probably chose Ted

Hughes or Charles Causley with 'Meet My Folks' and 'Figgie Hobbin'. At that actual moment, there was very little poetry for children that was truly autobiographical, as well as humorous and written from a child's point of view. At that time, I didn't see this as a 'gap in the market' or 'an unfulfilled children's need' but in retrospect that's what it looks like. Not that I am suggesting some explosion took place when that book or the next few came out. In that tiny world of children's poetry there was a bit of a ripple. And if ripples ruffle feathers, that's what happened, and over the years both the ripples and the ruffles have got bigger. I frequently arrive somewhere where a fellow writer or critic has just been and find that I am standing answering criticisms that he or she has made about me: 'He doesn't write *Poetry*'; 'he's just an entertainer', 'he's a lightweight', 'Like ice cream, you think in prospect you can take a lot more of it than you find, in the eating, you can manage...' (Charles Causley, Sandy Brownjohn and Aidan Chambers). I have therefore been put in the position of having to defend myself, as if somehow I've done something wrong, or that I'm a charlatan who has posed as one thing when really I'm another.

As a result, I have had to develop an argument that runs right from when these criticisms appeared until the writing of this book; an argument concerning poetry, children, writing, talking, culture and education.

Needless to say I have not done this in isolation, but as a result of working with hundreds of teachers since 1976. I hope that this book will be useful for teachers like them.

IV

Before diving into the main body of the book, there's one argument I would like to deal with here. The 'he-doesn't-write-poetry' number. For years, in the face of this I would say, 'Well, don't call it "Poetry" then, call it "Bits" or "Stuff", I'm not really bothered what you call it.' The issue

8

has always seemed to me to be pointless if all it involves is a question of whether you can be in a club or not.

The implication is that a 'poet' is writing something superior to something that is just set out to look like poetry. The word itself, 'poetry', is being used as the criterion for good or bad, not the actual nature of what I, or any other writer, is trying to say. We only need to make an analogous argument to see how absurd it is. If someone tells us a story, we don't usually tell her at the end that she was not singing very well. In other words, I've never really been bothered by having a name for what I write. Some people call them poems, sometimes I do, some people call them stories. I can see that, as a body of writing, my work is a rag-bag of styles and genres, according to orthodox literary criticism, but does it matter? I'm not trying to hoodwink anyone, I'm not trying to gain membership to a Peerage of Poets. I write 'Bits' and 'Stuff'.

Most of the time, I have been quite happy to leave the 'is-it-poetry?' debate with people who seem to need to worry about such things. But there is one part of me that never likes to run away from a fight, especially if it involves language and literature. One day, several years back I read W.H. Auden and John Garrett's introduction to the anthology 'The Poet's Tongue' written in 1935. (My italics.)

'Of the many definitions of poetry, the simplest is still the best; *'memorable speech.'* That is to say, *it must move our emotions or excite our intellect, for only that which is moving or exciting is memorable, and the stimulus is the audible spoken word and cadence,* to which in all its power of suggestion and incantation we must surrender, as we do when talking to an intimate friend ...

'*All speech has rhythm,* which is the result of the combination of the alternating periods of effort and the rest necessary to all living things and the laying of emphasis on what we consider important; and in

9

all poetry there is a tension between the rhythm due to the poet's personal values, and those due to the experiences of generations crystallised into habits of language such as the English tendency to alternate weak and accented syllables and conventional verse forms like the hexameter, the heroic pentameter or the French Alexandrine...

'Memorable speech then. About what? Birth, death and Beatific Vision, the abysses of hatred and fear, the awards and miseries of desire, the unjust walking the earth and the just scratching miserably for food like hens, triumphs, earthquakes, deserts of boredom and featureless anxiety, the Golden Age promised or irrevocably past, *the gratifications and terrors of childhood,* the impact of nature on the adolescent, the despairs and wisdoms of the mature, the sacrificial victim, the descent into Hell, the devouring and the benign mother? Yes, all of these, but not these only. *Everything that we remember no matter how trivial: the mark on the wall, the joke at luncheon, word games,* these like the dance of a stoat or the raven's gamble are equally the subject of poetry...

'Poetry is no better and no worse than human nature; it is profound and shallow, sophisticated and naive, dull and witty, bawdy and chaste in turn.

'In spite of the spread of education and the accessibility of printed matter, there is a gap between what is commonly called "highbrow" and "lowbrow" taste, wider perhaps than it has ever been....

'The "average" man (sic) says: "When I get home I want to spend my time with my wife or in the nursery; I want to get out on the links or go for a spin in the car, not to read poetry. Why should I? I'm quite happy without it." We must be able to point out to him that *whenever, for example, he makes a good joke he is creating poetry,* that one of the motives behind poetry is curiosity, the wish to

10

know what we feel and think, and how, as E.M. Forster says, can I know what I think till I see what I say, and that curiosity is the only human passion that can be indulged in for twenty four hours a day without satiety...

'Poetry is not concerned with telling people what to do, but with extending our knowledge of good and evil, perhaps making the necessity for action more urgent and its nature more clear, but only leading us to the point where it is possible for us to make a rational and moral choice.... one must overcome the prejudice that poetry is uplift and show that *poetry can appeal to every level of consciousness*... one must disabuse people of the idea that poetry is primarily an escape from reality. We all need escape at times, just as we need food and sleep and some escape poetry there must always be. One must not let people think either that poetry never enjoys itself, or that it ignores the grimmer aspects of existence.'

The collection made by Auden and his co-author John Garrett includes sea shanties, extracts from mummer's plays, gravestone epitaphs, John Ball's letter to fellow peasants during the Peasant's Revolt of 1382, an extract from the Book of Job, ballads, songs, nursery rhymes and what they call a 'Negro Folk Song'. There are poems by Mary Coleridge, Emily Dickinson, Jean Ingelow, Edith Sitwell, and Christina Rossetti. I would like to think I write 'memorable speech' and this book is about helping children write it too.

CHAPTER 1
Why Bother With 'Memorable Speech'?

The children we work and play with at home and at school are not blank pages. They have seen and done many things and people have done many things to them. The reasons why we should bother to get children doing some of the kinds of things I suggest later in this book lie in looking at what children do and say and what is done to them.

1. CHILDREN AND POWER

Part of the business of being a child is being not-powerful. We can all remember having to move house, move school, go on holiday to places we didn't like, visit relatives or friends we didn't like. There was nothing we could do about it — that's the way it was. At a deeper level, we also knew that parents brought food into the house, put clothes on us and looked after us when we were ill. At various times we had fears and worries that a parent or two would die and then what? At various times we defied parent figures, sometimes perhaps testing whether they really were bigger and stronger than us, because we knew ourselves how unable we were at fending for ourselves.

Many of the children I meet, in inner-city schools have further complications to this pattern. Poverty, migration, unemployment and the cutting back of the welfare state have had a devastating effect on children's lives. It's not just simply that they're hungry, though this is sometimes the case, but that the strains of not having money, of having to spend hours queuing for benefits, buses and health care takes its toll on the way we are with each other in personal relationships. Children, as the least powerful but seemingly the most needy, frequently become the butt of people's frustrations. Anyone who has worked with children like these knows that they know a lot but have no power to change their circumstances. There isn't even room for negotiation over whether you will or won't get a clip round the ear or what your chances are of getting another sweet.

2. CHILDREN AND 'REHEARSING'

A lot of what we ask children to do can be described as rehearsing. Combing your sister's hair is a 'real' activity, in the sense that you actually comb someone's hair. Combing Little Pony's hair is a 'rehearsal'. Copying pictures of cars is 'rehearsal', making a go-kart is 'real'. A lot of what we ask children to do in school are 'rehearsal' activities. Plotting graphs for experiments they have not carried out, would be an example. At home, quite a lot of children are shielded, by well-meaning parents, from having to make their own beds, wash up or choose their own clothes. We prevent them from taking part in what I call 'real' activities.

3. CHILDREN AND TV

This debate mostly goes on around the issue of the quality of TV, which neatly leaves out the issue of quantity. Many of the children I meet are sitting in rooms where a TV is on for over thirty hours a week.

Many people have shown that this activity is itself very passive; hand and eye co-ordination is down to zero; the narrative line of much of what they watch is totally realised in images, 'leaving nothing to the imagination', the rapid image changing technique of TV limits attention span in real life; TV presents a large amount of 'knowledge' that is in fact unusable because the TV watcher never gets round to trying it out; most of the human characters presented to the children are not ones they are themselves like — that is to say there are very few examples, in thirty hours of TV, of children saying and doing and thinking the things that the TV-watching child says, does and thinks. In addition to this list, I would add a mini-theory of my own. I think extensive TV-watching teaches children how to forget. The experience of watching four hours of TV forces the watcher to 'junk' whole hours. There is literally too much information to retain: information in the form of image, sound, movement, narrative line, idea or whatever. In fact, in order to get the most out of the moment you watch, it is quite a good idea not to deliberate on the moment that preceded it. These observations are made with reference to children who watch over four hours a night and more at weekends; that is, unselective, extensive watching.

4. SCHOOL AND CULTURE

The idea of school that most of us have is a place where children go to learn things. Children are people who don't know very much and so they are put in a classroom with people who know more. It is then the job of the people who know more, to transfer some of their knowledge to the child. This has been called the 'Jug-and-Mug' theory of education, where the teacher is the full jug, the child is the empty mug and the teacher's job is to pour knowledge from the full jug to the empty mug.

The main problem with this idea of education is that no child is an empty mug. Every child, no matter how young, comes to school with 'knowledge', or as I would prefer to call it, culture. The problem is that unless we ask them questions about this culture we never find out that it exists. Instead we spend our time initiating the children

14

into a school-based culture. A simple example I've observed is an occasion that happened when I was working with some fourteen-year-olds. The teacher had brought in playscripts of the film 'Gregory's Girl' for the class to read out. The lad who took the part of Gregory read reasonably well, other than that he kept missing his cue. The reason for this was that in actual fact he was more intent on performing the latest rapping lyrics he was perfecting under his breath. This illustration is not given in order to say that he should have been rapping INSTEAD of reading 'Gregory's Girl' but that he might have been given the chance and space at some time to read 'Gregory's Girl' AND do some rapping. His culture was irrelevant. With this in mind and as a result of working with children I have come up with an incomplete list that is meant to represent the components of a young person's culture. Each item stands for a set of questions that we might ask a school student: 'What do you do when... ?' 'What do you say when...?' 'Has your father ever said...?' and so on. When this book first came out I was working with the National Oracy Project with a view to fleshing out this list into materials that teachers would be able to use directly with children and older school students.

Fears
Dreams and nightmares
Tricks
Revenges
Trusted people
Thrills
In trouble
Accidents
Sadnesses, regrets
Prides
Shames
Mysteries, things I/we are mystified by
Vows, resolutions
Wishes and hopes

Rumours
Proverbs
Rhymes
Riddles
Games
Laws
Rules
Punishments
Sayings
Stories I've been told, by parents, relations, grand-parents, peer group
Happenings and events in the history of my cultural/ethnic group, class/national group
Jokes
Special days
Songs
Attitudes to other members of the family, family conversations and arguments
Mucking about, having a laugh, having a good time
Places we go, private/public places to meet and wait for each other, hanging about
Celebrations and feasts
Foods, favourite dishes and recipes
The 'way we do it': garden, hair, dress, style, habits
Hobbies, pastimes, pursuits, activities, crazes
Music, dance, song (participated, performed, spectated)
Sports: participatory/spectator
Kinds of work done by me (as a part-timer), or by parents/grandparents and relations, brothers and sisters, other people, as interviewed, housework, losing work, living without work, activities at work that are not work, like skiving, having a laugh, organising, strikes, break-times, knocking off
Courtship, marriage, weddings, divorces. Alternatives, like single parenting, gay relationships
Holidaying
Outings

Slangs, dialects, ingroup jargons and new words

Family sagas, stories

Street spectacles and events, as seen or participated in

Superstitions and charms

Oaths and secrets, about secret illicit deeds, for instance

Street cries, market traders, bus conductors

Local legends, myths, urban folk stories

It's not fair: wrong-doers, cheats, conmen, cruel people

Heroes, heroines, anti-heroes, local or historical

Victims and scapegoats — me or others, on the receiving end

Private matters, what I choose to be 'personal'

Irritating things, things that annoy

Attitude to physique — self and others — physical traits, body

Loyalties: taking sides, identifying with groups or individuals

Between two cultures: divided loyalty and identities

Battlegrounds: where and why — home/street/work

Clubs and organisations

Gender-determined activities — questioning this

Attitudes to change — could things be better for me/my cultural group/my family?

The future for me/imagined/for all of us

Death: opinions/observed/bereavement

Supernatural — afterlife, god, ghosts, other-life creatures, magic

Disasters: me/my family, my people

My room

Authority and control; attitudes to it — parent/school/outside

Fantasies — what if I was a...?/my imaginary helper/me as someone else, i.e. role play as victim, boss, other people; imaginary worlds: good, bad, futuristic

Gangs, mates, friends, rivals
Desertions and separations
Lovers and loved ones
Solidarity, not grassing, standing by mates/family/my people
Goings on in the attitudes to, institutions I belong in, like school, work place, block of flats, family
Neighbours
Responses to 'natural phenomena', weather, seasons, landscape
Pets
Parties
Encounters with strangers
Arguments, disputes, rows
Disappointments
Promises, made or broken
My moods
My beliefs/strong feelings, me on a soap box

(The list comes from an article about schools and children's culture in which I try to show children's culture and children's writing cannot be separated. It is printed in appendix I — page 91 in this book).

5. CHILDREN AND 'METALANGUAGE'

The word 'metalanguage' is used in many different ways. Here I use it in the sense meant by sociologist Henri Lefebvre in 'Everyday Life in the Modern World' (Allen Lane 1971). He wanted to describe the process by which we frequently talk or write about our own or other peoples' words. We have a whole area of study, linguistics, which is 'metalanguage'. We even do it in everyday speech when we say: 'what I mean to say is....' and we redefine what we've just said. However, Lefebvre was interested in looking at cultural phenomena where we have an appointed range of people in our society whose job it is to summarise, paraphrase, redefine and redescribe other people's words and experiences. The example he gives is of the tourist who goes to Venice and is unable to look at the Doge's Palace without reading the verbal commentary: 'didactic speech is interposed between works of art and their understanding'.

I have found it useful to apply this critique to much of the language experience and practice of children in schools. For example, I have watched many Educational TV documentary films that explain simple industrial processes to children: 'The Bakery', 'The Garage' and the like. One of these described the process of making sweets. On screen we saw a pair of hands passing sweets on to a conveyor belt, the commentator, (male) said: 'the sweets are put on to the conveyor belt.'

This utterance we take as normal 'objective' language, the kind that we want children to learn so that they can 'understand' processes, data, empirical phenomena. But it's not as simple as that. There are many ways in which we can 'understand' what is going on at this moment. For example, we could ask the camera person to pull out his/her focus and see who it is putting the sweets on to the conveyor belt.... and yes, it's a human being, and yes, it's a woman. Now we can ask the woman what she is doing, and she might say, 'I am putting the sweets on to the conveyor belt.' She might use a language particular to her job 'I tip/lob/fling/slip/heave' the 'sweets/mintdrops/candy/ stuff' on to the 'belt/line' or whatever. We would share with her the idiom of her work. But more important than that even, we could ask her what she thinks and feels about what she is doing. She might want to tell us that her back aches or that it's great to do a job because it gets her out of the home. Now, of course, 'factual language', 'objective language' tells us that such observations are irrelevant to the 'process' in question. But are they? In a humane society wouldn't we want to know, as part of the process, that a worker's back aches when she puts the sweets on to a conveyor belt? Isn't that part of the process too? We have it so ingrained into us that 'industrial process' and empirical language consist of removing observations of feeling and thought that we think that it is more 'correct'. We actually think that saying the sweets *are put* (passive mood, as they used to say in Latin Grammar lessons) is a more accurate way to describe what is going on.

Now, in case you think I am making a mountain out of a molehill here, take a look at the non-fiction books around you, watch the news, read the newspapers and you will see that we accept as normal that journalists, writers, commentators and the like can summarise and mediate and describe other people's experiences much better than the people themselves. The postman's job, in a little junior school text book is described by a writer who has never delivered a letter in his/her life, so again we are deprived of knowing what a postman thinks about it. One journalist asks another 'what is the mood in Beirut tonight?', 'what does the Prime Minister think about this?', 'what are people thinking about that?' and so on. The journalist tells us, quite often without a quotation at all.

As far as children are concerned, the consequences can be quite damaging. They spend large amounts of time reading and writing 'metalanguage' of this kind. This means that they neither engage with the authentic feelings and thoughts of others in the outside world, nor with other children in the class, nor with themselves, when they are working in the 'metalanguage mode'.

6. CHILDREN AND ORAL LANGUAGE

It is very difficult as an adult to remember how our knowledge becomes more and more based on written language. However, not only are there big differences in adult and child, there are also differences between adults. Those people who train for work using books and written language tend to differ in the way they use language from people who train for work orally and visually. The children of these two kinds of adults tend to differ accordingly.

In our classrooms we have children who are the most oral, namely the children of parents who trained for work orally, the less oral — children of parents who trained for work using books yet who are still as children, more oral than their parents.

Being oral means several things:

i) It means that many of the values you hold, come to you through what someone has said. Children have listened to parents talking about relatives and friends and listened to what parents have said about them and their goings on. Children have engaged with each other for hours debating what is fair, unfair, who is a good person, who is a bad one and so on.

ii) You develop a repertoire of idioms, jargon, phrasings, slang, formulae that are appropriate to the oral community you live in.

iii) It is likely you possess a set of anecdotes, stories, rhymes, songs, jokes that come to you through this oral community. (See the list on pages 15-18.)

iv) A large number of words and phrasings in our language come from the development of writing. Children come across these as spoken by adults, as read to them by adults or as they become initiated into the written language themselves. When children, or highly oral adults, hear words that they do not understand they perceive those words at their most physical, ie sound, tone, rhythm, and position in a cadence. This means that great possibilities for the absurd present themselves: words that sound like other words but mean something different, sequences of words that sound similar, breaking up words into bits and putting them together again, making up words and putting them into syntactically

21

correct positions and so on. All this we are very familiar with as 'childish babble', 'nonsense verse', tongue twisters, gobbledygook, sound poems and the like — much of which children do unprompted but which is also enriched by a literary tradition of more of the same. Language in this context is laughed at. Words that you would not expect to be put together are linked through rhyme or alliteration, rude and irreverent meanings are derived from putting words that sound similar into the 'wrong' context. There is a sense in which all this language use represents the voice of the confused getting it's own back, taking control of that seemingly powerful and dominating thing called adult language.

v) Many young children, or older semi-literate children and adults, do not really know that everything that they say can be represented in writing. They do not realise that their noises, grunts, shouts, whispers, slang, rude words, dialect phrasings and the like can actually be all written down.

Having looked at some characteristics of children and some influences on them, we are now in a position to consider how writing 'memorable speech' is a worthwhile activity. However, as any writer of a text like this knows, I have a problem here in that I want to show i) how it is worthwhile, and ii) how to go about doing it, both at the same time. After all, how can I prove that it is worthwhile unless I show exactly what is involved? The 'memorable speech' activities I am referring to come later in Chapter 3 if you want to turn to them now.

I would like to isolate three characteristics of the writing process that I think are important:

i) Writing is a way of *preserving* things, or as I say to children, it's like making a photo album. Of course it's not the only way to preserve things because memory is a

22

preserver, video and sound tapes are too. But there are unique features about writing as a preserver. The process of recording is actually quite slow, but it is cheap and portable, the direct opposite of the TV process, which is transient and disposable. When the writing concerned is personal, it has the potential of putting the writer centre-stage. It can help you deal with the world that seemingly you have little control over. A writer can play god with his/her characters in a fiction but he/she can also manipulate real people (including him/herself). Because the process of writing involves putting experience down on the space in front of you, it gives you the time and space to change what you have done. This is not merely a technical game but offers the writer the potential of seeing how writing involves selection and manipulation of experiences, thoughts and ideas. This means control and power. Writing also offers the possibility of being a 'real' activity and not a rehearsed one. This involves being authentic to one's own experience and ideas, more of which later.

Because writing preserves, it is a very convenient way to preserve the oral tradition. It can't do it with all its vigour and context, but it can do it quite well. It can record playground songs, stories my grandad told me, a tongue twister my friend told me, funny things our dads say when they stand in front of the mirror. It can represent dialect, monologue, dialogue, jokes, commands, pleadings, intimate chats and gossip. Much of this is a highly undervalued, uncherished area of human creativity. It exists as the main carrier of our culture and identity, and yet children in schools get very few chances to record it and celebrate it. (See the list on pages 15-18.) Writing it does give them that possibility.

But it is more valuable than that: because this oral output is wrapped up in personal identity, it exists in a continuum with 'personal thoughts'. If we want children to write thoughtful, authentic personal writing then they will want to be sure that we are genuinely interested in who they are. It is my experience that this involves talking and recording things like: accounts of trips to the mosque, 'how we do weddings', rules of playground games, slang words for getting told off, complaining, playing truant, being a coward, a bully etc. The act of preserving this kind of thing gives a believable context for personal writing. It also links writing about personal things to the oral power that children already possess. (See later Oral Writing.) Because I regard this continuity between the oral tradition and personal writing as being so important I have put material on this in Appendix I.

ii) Writing is a way of *reflecting* on experience and ideas. When this is personal, true experience, a unique phenomenon takes place: I put a piece of myself down on a page in front of me and I can look at it. The experience is no longer buzzing around in my head waiting to come out: it is there on the page for me to look at. And it's me! I can now make comparisons between the written experience and how I remembered it before I wrote it. I become both a participant and an observer. Paradoxically, having written about something *subjectively,* I can now be more objective about it for a moment or — as is more likely — move between the two positions: 'I did that... was I like that?... I was a fool to do that... was I fool to do that? Anyone who would do a thing like that must be a fool... I didn't think I was a fool then but I think now it was foolish of me to have done that ...' And so on.

However, to go back a bit in the actual process of writing, the very act of trying to get a remembered experience right in writing, very often involves discoveries. Most writing forces us to be linear, putting one event, thought, feeling or idea after another. Given also that the process of getting it down on the page is physically slow, what often happens is that the writer discovers aspects of the experience that lay hidden, half remembered, or unthought-out.

As a result of all these kinds of reflections the relationship between me and that experience changes. Moreover, I am partly aware that I have done the changing myself. In a very small way, I have shown to myself that the world is not simply passively received (like TV) but a place that I can help shape. All very lofty stuff, perhaps, but for me, it is the pole star I am using to guide me in what to write, why write, what to get children to write, and how to get them to write.

iii) Writing is a way of opening up a *conversation* of a specific kind because it is potentially one based on personal reflection of the kind I have just described. Of course all oral conversations can be frivolous or 'deep' as we choose. However, in classrooms, we know that it is frequently very difficult to slow things down enough to get children to reflect slowly and carefully, and then to share their reflections with each other. Sharing writing is a way of doing this. It is one way in which we can take children seriously. All those 'silly childish things' like being jealous of one's brother, or not liking housework can be dealt with as real experiences of that human stage called childhood. By treating it as real and valid now, we acknowledge that the child is not simply a pre-adult with incomplete or immature feelings. We give the child the possibility of valuing his or her own experience.

By *preserving, reflecting and opening conversations* with each other, children can begin to situate themselves in relation to each other with a lot more information. They now know, perhaps, what their grandads do, or how Sadia's mum ran away from home. At a personal level they can begin to evaluate their own experience against another person's. It is a vital part of learning 'who I am' to know 'am I the only person in the world who...?' or, as is more likely, 'you mean... as well?' Sharing culture and sharing personal experience opens up the possibilities of cooperation, mutual respect and real friendships. It can be a strong foundation from which alternatives to 'metalanguage' can be launched.

Much of the debate about literacy is focussed on the 'can' principle. 'Can he read?' 'Can she write?' I am more interested in the questions does he read, does she write?

Are people who leave school, who can but don't read or write, really literate? I am interested in a practice in schools that leads people to want to read and write regardless of whether they are 'successes' or 'failures' as regards exams. With this in mind, I want in the next chapter to look a little more closely at the process of writing.

CHAPTER 2
Writing and the 'Written Mode'

If I write 'Wow, that's fantastic', that represents something I could say and indeed do say. If I read this piece of narrative prose:

> 'But Gilda was no simpleton. She knew with some exactness how long an employer like Miss Graf could tolerate her. When the soup was cold, the saucepan boiled dry, the wedding silver tarnished, the bone china cracked, Miss Graf would with regret cast Mrs Blacksmith and her bastard back on the public care.'
> ('The Chant of Jimmie Blacksmith' by Thomas Keneally)

I know that it is something that *can* be spoken but would not actually be said in everyday speech. It is, in passing, quite interesting to speculate why not. Is it the measured length of the structures; the fact that structures get repeated in a certain way; the matching adjectives; the plopping in of adverbial phrases? Or perhaps it's the over-all construction of the paragraph which is, in a sense, conceived backwards. The writer knows that the climax is the likelihood of Miss Graf throwing Mrs Blacksmith plus bastard out. Everything that comes before is a carefully layered hypothesis. In speech, we rarely manage such a structure, where we hold back a punch line for so long.

I am drawing a distinction here between one kind of writing that can and does represent *said phrases and expressions* and another that is in the 'written mode'.

Most children over the age of seven are asked to write in 'the written mode'. They are asked to write things that they don't actually say. Some children of 'low ability' can never learn the written mode, while many other children pick it up so quickly they forget they ever did or could write in an 'oral mode'. What is happening here, is that we are initiating children into the act of writing without taking full notice that we're asking them to engage in a kind of translation. If a child's language is, in many key areas, very different from the standard written language, then the word 'translation' really applies. For example, the correct cockney way to say 'I haven't got any' is 'I ain't got none'. Many questions that cockney children ask end with the phrase 'innit?' even if the subject of the sentence is 'I'. 'I'm going out, innit?' (see 'DIALECT' page 61).

When we bear in mind the extent and nature of children's oral culture, then this business of the relationship between 'written mode' and 'oral mode' writing and what it means to them, is very important. (See Appendix I.)

Consider this:

THE MAGPIE AND THE VITAMIN
When I was four
Daddy and I were driving
in the car when
Daddy saw a magpie in
the bush, so he got
out of the car and he
picked it up and gave it
me to hold. We drove
home.
We asked my friend
Kate for her crow cage.
When Mummy saw it
she gave it two drops
of vitamins. In the morning
I accidentally gave it two

spoons of vitamins. The next
morning it was dead.

   So we held a
funeral for it. We
wrapped it up in an
old napkin and buried
it under a wattle tree
near the graves of a
chook* and a rooster
and of our dogs,
Tristan and Isolde.

* chicken (Australian)

This was written as a result of Graves/Walsh 'Process Writing' work and has been shown to me as an example of fine children's writing. Fine writing? Hang on. Of course it is all correct, well sequenced: there's a beginning, middle and end — BUT where's the feeling? You saw a magpie? What did you *think?* You held a magpie when you were four? What did it *feel* like? What did you *say?* What did you *think?* You gave it two spoonsful of vitamins? What do you *think* about that now? It died? What did you say about that? What did Dad *say?* What did you *think?* A funeral? Did anyone sing? Did you say a prayer? Did you cry?

   In fact, on seeing this piece of writing, I want to know what kind of 'education' is it that produces such 'perfect writing', so devoid of feelings about things of such importance to a child?

   Look at the first sentence, with its six clauses. First of all there's the establishing information of 'when I was four' and 'Daddy and I'. Children are being told to do this so that they widen the circle of their audience. As a process, it immediately puts children on their guard, they're having to concentrate on the written mode of describing an event. The story suddenly ceases to be theirs. We're in the business of the jug and mug theory of education. As you go through the piece, there are many

29

examples of this sometimes producing things that are almost ridiculous:

'When Mummy saw it, she gave it two drops of vitamins.' Really? Did Mummy just see it one moment, and the next, stick vitamins in its mouth? The child has been made self-conscious about her structures and sequencing. There are also examples of the hyper-correct. 'I accidentally gave it' 'and of our dogs' 'and buried' 'our dogs, Tristan etc.'

Let's look at the model of writing that was used here:

---

1 Pre-Writing

---

i EXPERIENCE OF A PROBLEM	ii PRE-WRITING
decision to write; growth of intention	thinking; incubation; talking; rehearsing; discussing; reading; researching; note-taking writing

---

2 Writing

---

iii DRAFTING	iv REVISING (authorial)
doodling; brainstorming; splurging; planning;	adding; cutting; reordering; clarifying;

writing;
reading;   v EDITING
reflecting;   (secretarial)
collecting;
connecting.   correcting;
                         proof reading
                         for punctuation
                             spelling
                             grammar
                             rewriting

---

3 Post Writing

---

vi PUBLICATION   vii READER'S   viii WRITER'S
                      RESPONSE   ATTITUDE

Appropriate
format:
                                    reflecting
                                    on the whole
article   experience.
book
card
letter
newspaper

Under 'pre-writing', all sounds fine — there's a good
chance that at this stage, all the real emotions and feelings
plus the memories of *what people said* are swimming
around. It's in the next three stages that something goes
wrong. Instead of finding ways to represent what we say
and what we think (see page 37) the child has to 'plan', 're-
order' and 'cut'. The real problem is that this process sets
up expectations. Children at this age are often keen to
please and so they struggle to get their stories into this

31

kind of shape. They learn the conventions of written-mode writing but at what price? And so young. The end result is a kind of 'metalanguage' about self. Even the ritualistic titling: 'The Magpie and the Vitamins', is impersonal. The chances are this anecdote already existed in the girl's head as 'something awful I once did', or some other convention of *conversation,* when she'd told the story to friends or family.

Now here's something that has been shown to me as an example of 'bad writing':

It was a summer day when my
father and I were going to the shops
when this car came
to tern and the lit was red and
dad just went and of cause
bang. There was a crash. My
dad and the man step out of the
car dad started to talk
loudly. The man said look
it all happen quickly so
ask your kid. Glenda said will
I'm telling you the true dad it's
your fall 'what' you went
on a red light.

The interesting thing about this piece is that the child *starts* to write in the approved 'Process' way.* He is well-initiated, but not well enough.

For whatever reasons, his oral mode breaks through: 'the lit was red and dad just went and of cause bang'. Or, as I would show a kid how to lay it out: (see Free Verse section page 37)

* 'Father and I', 'It was... when... when'

'The light was red
and dad just went.
And of course — BANG!'

The subject of the story is as 'important' as the magpie
story is, a kid 'shaming up' her dad in public, a car crash,
and breaking the law, but this time the meaning of the
story is carried in *dialogue,* with the result that we get a
graphic and emotional picture instead of a dead reported
one. Again, as I would help a kid lay it out: (see Free Verse
page 37)

'Glenda said,
Well, I'm telling the truth, dad,
it's your fault.
WHAT!?!
You went on a red light.'

In other words, I would validate the oral mode, so instead
of the kid learning that he's written a bad piece, he could
learn that the way of writing was welcome and successful
(see 'Publishing and Performing', pages 82-85). Then who
knows what else he might write, or for that matter *how*
else?

Instead I can imagine this piece of writing processed and
conferenced into:

The Car Crash

It was a summer day when my father and I were going
to the shops when a car came to turn. The light was red
but dad [my father?] just went, so of course there was
a crash. My dad and the man stepped out of the car and
dad started to talk loudly.

The man said, 'Look, it all happened so quickly, so
ask your kid.'

My sister, Glenda, said, 'Well I'm telling the truth,
Dad, it's your fault.'

Dad said, 'What?'

'You went on a red light,' Glenda said.

33

What the lad would now know is that he is wrong; writing about this episode is a drag, demoralising and a waste of time, and, of course, that he is a 'failure'. It is in this way that the teaching of 'writing' becomes part of a conditioning process. It becomes more important that the writer is 'correct' and behaving according to norms than that he or she should write the truth. Any of us who has had any experience in school knows, the moment we read this boy's piece, that he is an example of why working class children fail in schools. We know that by all of the criteria available in schools (as they are), the kid is a 'failure'. And yet, as I hope I've shown, the piece is actually evocative, true to the boy's culture, authentic and therefore 'good'.

By comparing these two pieces of writing, we can see how easy it is for 'good' writing to prevent children (and the adults they become) from writing expressively. Fear of not being able to write 'properly' may also cut them off from writing at all. A better way is to encourage all children to write expressively in the voice they possess: the oral voice. The problem starts right on entry to schools when slogans are put up under pictures like 'This is my dog.', when in actual fact the child never said 'This is my dog'. The child may have said, 'It looks like my dog but it ain't', but how often would anyone write *that* under a picture? I would like to claim here that children need to discover that *exactly what they say* can be represented on the page right from the very start. They need to carry on doing that among the other kinds of writing they learn as they get older. In this way children will have a foundation of literacy based on the competence they already possess: their oral language. Getting all children to work in the written mode from the start and all the time is quite clearly not working. I am suggesting this as an alternative.

I propose here an alternative to the Graves/Walsh one.

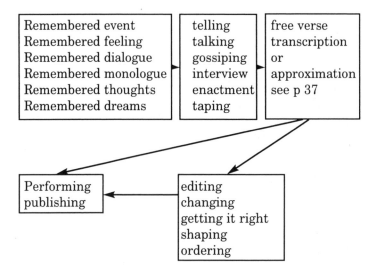

Complementary to this is the same model with the word 'imagined' substituted for 'remembered'.

I make 'remembered' a priority because children all possess memories as their own oral knowledge. The creating of imagined events, feelings and the like is a different creative process and I am not sure in my own mind it should be forced into 'oral mode' writing, although it should be borne in mind that calling up memories and imagining events are closely related activities for many children.

An expansion of the model is necessary to include the oral forms that children already possess (see Appendix I) and the fact that children perceive language at its most physical.

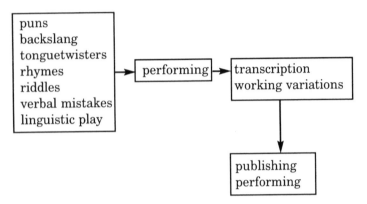

And that model can be seen as part of this:

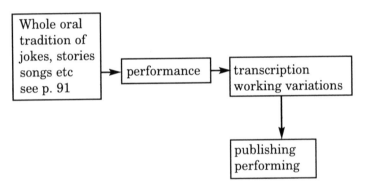

CHAPTER 3
Starting Points for Oral Writing

1 FROM THE POINT OF VIEW OF FORM

i Free Verse

Free verse is a way of writing things down in a way that helps someone to read it in the way you want them to. It is a kind of musical notation. What I say to children is:

'SLOW!
Children crossing'

means something different from

'Slow children crossing.'

I might show them this poem by e e cummings:

Buffalo Bill's

Buffalo Bill's
defunct
        who used to
        ride a watersmooth-silver
                                stallion
and break onetwothreefourfive pigeonsjustlikethat
                                        Jesus
he was a handsome man
                        and what i want to know is
how do you like your blueeyed boy
Mister Death

Alternatively, I ask children to invent ways of representing the following on the page:
1 A word or phrase said loudly.

2 A word or phrase said quickly.
3 A single word said very slowly, as we do when we call out for mum(!).
4 A phrase said slowly as if we were thinking between each word.
5 Some words or numbers said to a rhythm.
6 Several phrases written down in such a way that they represent the way we pause between phrases. Take for example, what you actually say when you recount what you did when you got up this morning.

If the children have big pieces of paper, and plenty of colours, this kind of examination of ways of representing the spoken word on the page can take a good few hours. The walls can be covered with them and so there is plenty of room for debate about which method of representation works the best. Many children invent new ways to do it. I tell them, if it works, then it's OK. There is no one way that is right, or best. In this way, they are already in charge of the writing process. They are making up rules as they go along.

I probably won't use the word 'poetry' at all but I have put the discussion of what can be written, into the oral area. What we are going to write will be 'oral' because I am describing ways of writing things down that reflect the way we say things. I call it 'Oral Writing'.

Then I say two more things: Write down what people *say* and write down what you *think*.

These may seem really obvious tips to give children but in fact it works out that it's not so obvious as all that. For a variety of reasons, children quickly grow accustomed, when writing about themselves, in school, to reduce their experiences to reported speech or externally observed descriptions of internally experienced events (as in the story 'The Magpie and the Vitamins', or, as in something like this: 'Mum was angry, so I went to my room.') In the face of writing like this, or in anticipation of it, I say 'What did mum actually *say* when she was angry?' Well, maybe it went something like this; says the child:

> 'If there's any more trouble from you, you'll get a clip round the ear, I'm sick and tired of it, I tell you.'

So I say, if that's the sort of thing she says, write it down. Then I say, 'what did you *think* after your mum said that?' Well, maybe it went something like this; says the child:

> 'Oh no, here she goes again, why doesn't she pick on Dave, he's horrible. He's got spots. He never gets into trouble. But I didn't say anything. I just went off to my room.'

Now, 'Mum was angry, so I went to my room.' turns into:

> Mum said:
> If there's any more trouble from you
> you'll get a
> CLIP ROUND THE EAR.
> I'm sickandtiredofit,
> I tell you.
> I thought
> OH NO
> Here she goes again
> why doesn't she pick on Dave?
> he's HORRIBLE
> he's got spots
> he never gets into trouble
>
> But I didn't say anything

```
I just went
        off
            to
                my
                    room.
```

My point in asking children to write down what people say
and what they themselves think, is that this is knowledge
they already possess. It isn't something they have to con-
coct or translate. Poetry has been described as 'the best
words in the best order.' But whose best? The teacher
might think that Keats is best and the child who approxi-
mates Keats in his or her poems is the 'best'. This then
leads into that well-known poetry writing method:
"Think-of-a-nice-word-to-describe-night."

Samantha:	Gloomy
Teacher:	Lovely
David:	Dark
Teacher:	Yes
Maureen:	Smelly
Teacher:	No, Maureen
Maureen:	But my sister's feet smell at night, miss.
Teacher:	No Maureen, smelly is not a nice word to describe night.

And the 'best order' approach leads teachers to follow the
Sandy Brownjohn method, outlined in her book 'Does it
have to rhyme?'

Teacher:	Right, class, here is a sonnet, a ballad and a haiku. Write one each and I'll come round and help you.
David:	What shall we write about?
Teacher:	A sonnet is good for describing something and saying what you think about it. A bal-lad is good for telling a story and a haiku is good for a glimpse at something.
David:	But what shall we write about?

The best-order, best-words approach is to my mind fairly pointless because inevitably it starts out from adult literary notions of what 'best' means. Both approaches involve the child in a writing process which they have to learn. Once again, teacher has the knowledge, the better judgement and better taste; the pupil is the blank, the empty mug. We need to find forms that *release* children's knowledge, liberate it and so give the child a sense of his or her own power. Free verse presentation of what people say and what you think, is one starting point in this process.

ii) Forms Within Free Verse

It's obvious that a lot of what gets called Free Verse isn't all that 'free'. That is to say there are patterns of phrasing, repetitions, perhaps the odd rhyme thrown in and so on. Now, of course it is possible to lead children to a poetic form and say; 'Write a poem like this.' And sometimes, in specific conditions, I would do this (see page 129). However when children are writing for truth and authenticity, I'd much rather let them invent their own forms, even if I know and you know that they are only re-inventing the wheel, or half-remembering something you read to them last week.

The important point here is that, the inventor has the experience of inventing, and the rest of the class has the experience of hearing an equal, a classmate, doing the inventing. My role, as teacher, at this point is to make sure I expose the other kids to that invention. Here is an example of a girl who has been introduced to Free Verse as I have presented it above, and pointed in the direction of writing something about herself, and something that people say to her.

> Growing.
> Who's growing?
> Not me.
> There goes Tiny Tina

41

I hear the children say
Growing
Who's growing?
Not me.

Tina.

A child invents a form. Perhaps, at some chatty moment we might discuss the repetition of the poem. Does it make it sound more plaintive? More naggy? More complaining? What about the one-liner of a comment about her: 'There goes Tiny Tina.' *You* can write poems that just pick up on just one thing that people say and what you think about it....

Now, without saying: 'You can write like Tina,' we can expect, in a class, some formal experiment, mimicry and variation to develop. In this way, the children share their subjective experiences in their writing but more — they take the shapes those subjective experiences have been put into by others and re-use them for themselves. They internalise the abstract aspect of poetry (the form) and then use it for themselves. What is important here, though, (unlike the 'let's write a sonnet' approach) is that the abstract (the form) arises out of the subjective (Tina's feelings). When Abdul or Maria (or whoever) decides to write, using repetition and framing (like Tina) he or she is taking the abstract from a known subjective source. Abdul and Maria have relationships with Tina. They don't with a book.

On a point of literary theory here, I don't accept, in the final analysis, a separation of 'subjective experience' and 'abstract form', nor do I say they are indivisible. But rather that we are only able to separate the two in our minds as an act of logic. In the reality of reading or writing the 'way something is written' and 'what is written' interact with each other in our consciousness. Philosophically, it is 'Idealism' to ask children to simply imitate form. To imitate form in the cultural context of a class and in the specific context of a classmate's subjective experience, is holistic. In the concrete reality, Abdul or Maria's pick-up from Tina will not simply involve the abstract form but also aspects of analogous subjective experience, like being black or hungry. Sadly, I don't have an example here, as this was a school I was later excluded from — my own children's!

iii Using Other People's Forms
And now to contradict some of the things I have just been saying.

There are times when it is appropriate to use a book-author's form and say to children, You can write like that.

I happen to think that the best times for this are when we're writing nonsense, rhyme, word play and the like, where the subjective content is of less importance. What we want here is the pleasure of the absurd, the incongruous juxtaposition of ideas, eg: through rhyme.

> I walked down the road
> and met a fat ????

What we get here, is a kind demolition of the real world of tables and chairs into 'dongs with luminous noses' or perhaps people sitting on tables and eating off chairs.

Within this area, children already possess a repertoire of forms, rude rhymes, skipping rhymes, clap games, football chants and for older children: rapping, toasting, country and western, rockabilly, soul, heavy metal and the whole gamut of pop forms. I'm interested in children getting to realise that language doesn't have to seem like A Thing; something that doesn't belong to you; or something that isn't part of how you *think*. Rather, it is a way of thinking you can control. Of course, language doesn't actually control anyone. Only people can do that. The sign: PRIVATE KEEP OUT, was put there by *someone*. We say 'the sign controls us', as a kind of shorthand. With children, we do something similar. We demand children write and perform language tasks that, metaphorically, tie them up in chains.

Language starts to seem like an external object you are supposed to acquire.

So let's give children the opportunity to be fluent and playful with words. One of the routes to fluency is through Free Verse.

However, in the context of nonsense, rhyme and word play we can give children the opportunity to perceive language at its most physical. We are saying, look, you can play with words just like you can play with sand or clay. And they can and will.

But let's remember several things: First of all it's a different process from free verse writing-for-truth, and so for children to get the full benefit from the two areas of writing I say, 'Keep the two kinds separate but keep *both* kinds going.' Ban rhyme when we're writing for truth (for children under ten). I don't believe children under ten can ever really tell the authentic truth about their own experiences and make it rhyme. Probably for the same reason that children of that age can't and don't handle other kinds of abstractions. So, help them find rhymes, rhythms and metres when they're writing the absurd. Let them demolish reality, let them voice unconscious anxieties about the real world by making a space where unlikely combinations of thoughts can sit side by side because the rhyme or rhythm says it's OK to do so. Of course, 'voicing unconscious anxieties' is a kind of truth and the separation I have made between 'writing for truth' and 'playing with words' is a false one. It's merely a convenience to avoid facetiousness and junk when we want true feeling. 'Let's have facetiousness and junk tomorrow.' Later, I explore how we can get children to play with words so that they sound like the thing that the words describe, ie: a fusion of 'playing with words' and 'writing for truth'.

So, to be specific; show children Lear, Milligan, West; remind them of the forms they already possess and make a space for them to have a go at working the variations. I, personally, find it tedious to use forms that were invented for humour and nonsense for saying 'important things'. I am thinking of things like Acrostic poems that say something 'deep'. However, some people get away with it so maybe it's worth a try sometimes...?

2 FROM THE POINT OF VIEW OF SITUATION

i Anecdotes

One of the least rated activities in schools is the telling of anecdotes — often relegated to the status of gossip or chat. It's what goes on before we ask a class to be quiet. I see anecdotes as the building blocks of our identity. Or, rather, they are the views of those building blocks. An event takes place in our lives, we choose to remember it. We relate it.

event . . . . . forgotten
event → remembered → related
event . . . . . forgotten

What makes us remember and/or relate an event? Because we recognise its significance: it still hurts, it still embarrasses, it still shocks us, other people remind us of it, other people have found it funny/interesting/significant/sad in the past. Perhaps, it still bothers us, perhaps, someone has just told us a story and we tell ours as comparison, or to outdo his or hers. Perhaps, we relate it in order to illuminate what's going on as awful warning, funny sidelight, friendly advice etc.

Anecdote-keeping (in our brain) and anecdote-relating are a vital part of everyday life. Everybody does it, every day. The incident chosen to *remember* is significant in relation to our identities and personalities. How and when we choose to tell others is similarly significant.

Every child we come across is full of anecdotes. This store exists as part of his or her oral knowledge. It is crucial to their identities and yet very very rarely do we ask children to represent their oral relating of these anecdotes on paper or in performance or both.

I suggest we should. The Free Verse form gives us the ideal way of representing these anecdotes.

So, how do we make anecdote-telling a starting point?

1) Teacher-based

You tell a story about something that happened to you. How you once stole something from a store, how you once burnt down the tool shed, how you once cut your brother's hair, how you once put on your mum's lipstick etc etc.

I'm being specific here because I'm both surprised and saddened by the way some teachers do one of the following:

A) Not reveal anything of themselves to a class and try to present themselves as a kind of impersonal teaching machine. (This never fools the kids who do a lot of homework speculating about who or what the teacher actually is.)

B) Tell anecdotes about themselves as a filler, a time-waster, as something to be done before getting on with something important.

The point is that if education is to mean anything at all, experiences have to be *felt*. As far as kids are concerned we know that that means discovering, experimenting, and creatively expressing experience. However, when we are confronted with someone else's felt experience, it has the capacity to engage us. We can relate to the substance of the experience and the person. We can engage with the substance by engaging with the person.

As an ideal starting point to get children to look at their own experiences, a teacher telling an anecdote can't be beaten. It's better than all the books that suggest five hundred ways of writing a poem. You tell them something that actually happened to you and then show them how such stories can be represented in the way that one *says* them. You can then chuck away the how-to-write-in-ten-easy-lessons books.

Out of your story, arise a variety of possibilities, the relevant reply, the tangential comment, the fantasy. Reap the harvest, get them down on tape, on paper, dictated, however. Make the writing part of the conversation. Make writing a way of having a conversation with people.

2) Child-based

A child tells us a story. Every day this happens and yet the stories disappear into thin air so that we can get on and do something else... like wondering what to write about. In schools, we have an uncanny knack of ignoring what's under our noses so that we can get on with what's more important. My son came home from school one day and said Leroy had been sent home. I said, why? He said, He punched Keith. Why did he punch Keith? Because Keith called him a black bastard. Did Keith get sent home too? Oh yes. (End of story.)

What a moment! Here in microcosm is all that you might ever want to talk about in school to do with racism, personal relationships, justice, equality, systems of punishment, discipline in institutions. There might be termfuls of writing and projects about immigration, slavery, what parents say to kids about other cultural groups, use of language and register of language and so on. Just because it was Keith who called Leroy a black bastard and it was Leroy who punched Keith doesn't mean it applies to them only, does it? It's happening all over the school, the city, the country and the world. Why? It's happening inside all of us. And yet here is this ideal and crucial 'educational moment' and it's gone. 'Discipline' is imposed — (whose discipline? on whose side?). And the moment vanishes. (Though of course the moment doesn't go really. The hidden curriculum, the real nitty-gritty of education, educates away like mad in moments like these and everyone goes off in their corner with their lesson learnt. What has Leroy learnt? What has Keith learnt? What have the other kids learnt? What has the teacher learnt?)

47

I once watched a film of a lesson in a Chinese school. In fact it wasn't a 'lesson' as we understand it. One of the kids had been nicking the other kids' stuff and so the class was discussing what should be done about it. I think we should do the same. 'Justice', 'fairness' or whatever is not really learnt out of books, but it can be learnt, in the here and now. Let's not 'rehearse' it, as people waiting to be adults, let's learn it now.

With children's anecdotes, of course, it may be literally impossible to deal with it, that second, that minute: so put it in cold storage. Ask Rashid to tell the same story later, ask him to put it on tape that second and we'll play it back later — he doesn't really have to go to assembly *that* moment, does he?

So then we listen to Rashid's anecdote. Again, what happens in the discussion? People make observations, comparisons, parallels, tangents. We find ways of getting it down. Grab the oral, represent it on the page, one-liners, speeches, thoughts, the whole lot.

3) Event-based

Just as teachers and pupils are great resources of anecdote, so is the institution of school itself. The raw event takes place in school, the felt experience takes place then and there: someone stole some money, someone was rude to someone else, someone ran out of school. Quick, let's discuss it. The issues that really matter to children will all be there. Why did she run out of school? What will she do? What should the school do? What would your parents say? Why are schools compulsory? What would you do instead of school? Why her? What should *we* do?

Then again, schools are sites where 'natural' events take place: dogs run into playgrounds, a tree falls down, there's a leak in the roof. Grab the event, talk about it. Write the talk down.

ii Dreams, Daydreams and Fantasies

I'll state the obvious: children daydream, dream and fantasise. We don't actually need to come in with adult-constructed fantasies by Edward Lear, Enid Blyton or Michael Rosen to get them to do so. Children don't *have* to imitate anyone else. I'm amazed at the way education books, poetry writing books, are full of suggestions to children and teachers about what to dream, daydream or fantasise about. As any observer of human beings will tell us, we can't escape from our fantasies, we can't stop ourselves dreaming and daydreaming. In order to get children to tell us about them, we don't have to make suggestions about what to dream, we only have to devise ways in which 1) they can remind themselves of the dreams, and 2) think they're worth telling anyone else.

Because our adult heads are so besotted with the adult-constructed fantasies we put in front of children eg: Films, Fairy Stories (I love them), we frequently try to get children to construct similar fantasies. The problem is that those films and fairy and folk stories often arose out of very different social and personal circumstances from the ones that the children live in. We might ask them to write stories about dragons and fairies. Are they *really* archetypes? Do they really reverberate in the children's fantasy world, unconscious, sub-conscious? Do they really have a 'physic reality'? (ie: the characters may be unreal but the emotions are real eg: fear). There are no cut and dried answers to these questions. It just depends. All I can say is that I'm rather suspicious of the 'write a poem about a dragon' approach (as asked of my son in school). Children are imagining like crazy all the time; what if Mum died? what if I wasn't hungry? what if I didn't have to go to school? They dream about all sorts of things: like food eating them, falling off high buildings, meeting a dead granny, and so on. They daydream about the people around them; they take themselves off to other places. If you made a Dream Book and everyone wrote down their dreams; if you made a Day-dream book in the same way; if you had a time in the week when everyone could talk freely about 'what-if...' and these got written down, no teacher would have to worry too much about thinking up topics for poems like 'Dragons' and 'Elephants-with-Wings'. And one child's dream, daydream and fantasy can spark off another twenty. Other children might want to take off from Maureen's dream about being swallowed by a pork pie and make up a mad story. The starting point is the telling of dreams, daydreams and fantasies (all ones that are really taking place). We find ways to orally transcribe them. We then have books full of 'fantasy writing'.

iii The 'Project'

Many kinds of so-called 'project work' involve children in not learning anything much more than how to copy things out of books. The ideas, the language, the approach — everything can be second hand but the project can look and sound wonderful, ie well copied out. So in the context of this book, I am assuming that project work will involve any or all of the following: original observation by children, experimentation, discovery, cross-referencing of ideas and information between people, books, films, and the original observations. In these ways, the project isn't some slab of useless knowledge that looks good, but a web of ideas that the child has really interacted with. For this to be possible, there has to be interaction between children in relation to what they are discovering and observing; and there has to be interaction with other *people,* eg: a postman, a visiting drama group or whatever. In this way, children learn that ideas don't exist in a metaphysical bubble that lives between the pages of books, but are part of the material reality of all human beings' consciousness. A lot of project work I've seen, treats knowledge as if it belongs to clever people called writers of encyclopedias. That's 'Book-knowledge' or 'Your-knowledge'. It only becomes

'My-knowledge' when it becomes ideas that affect me, ideas I can use, ideas that change me. That's why I have to observe, discover, experiment and talk to people. 'My-knowledge' in this way is made up of many kinds of 'Other-people's-knowledge'. 'My-knowledge' is a kind of 'My-our-knowledge'.

In the context of these kinds of things going on, some meaningful writing can take place. So, while the children are observing, discovering or experimenting, we don't have to be hidebound by the genres of scientific or topographical observation. It can be someone's job to record what people actually say: The 'cor blimeys', the 'ugh it smells', the 'what did you have for tea last night?' 'Observational writing' doesn't have to be the sacred cow of 'metalanguage'. It doesn't necessarily help the children *understand* anything better. Is the statement 'The snail is brown' any more significant than 'I don't like snails'? What's wrong with saying both things at the same time. 'The snail is all brown, I don't like it.'?

In the area of history, we are forever asking children to write things like 'The Vikings were a war-like people' which is either just copied out of a book, or copied out of a teacher's mouth. (And it may well be a lie anyway.) The Vikings had a literature and artifacts that the children can see, hear, and talk about. Any child can get to 'understand' the Vikings as well as any university professor, if given the opportunity to relate to the specifics in front of him/her. For example, out of Danish/Anglo-Saxon culture we've got 'Beowulf'. So let's say, as part of 'Project Viking' we look at the Viking longship (Brit. Mus.? a model?); we all sit down on the floor and row; go and look at some bit of landscape where a Viking could have once stood; we eat and drink and try to grow things that Vikings ate and drank and grew. Now, let's say we read 'Beowulf'. And now let's say we do drama improvisations from the story, like the scene where we wait for Beowulf to come up from the lake after fighting with Grendel's mother, or the scene back at Heorot while they're waiting for Beowulf and the others to come back. And now let's say we ask the children to write things like: 'I am Grendel's mother...' or 'I am a warrior...' Now, in this way, the children are in a situation where there is a free flow between emotional and so-called factual information. They use what they *know* to express what they *feel*.

I have chosen 'The Vikings' as an example here, not because I think 'The Vikings' is a great project but simply because, in England, it's become everyone's favourite topic.

In any school's locality, there are a hundred and one 'topics' that can be originally researched, (observed-experimented-discovered-discussed-people interviewed) just as 'exciting' as the Vikings, and the process by which the children find out about it can be that much more authentic. In this way, the children's writing can be about the world they live in, and how it came to be the way it is, how people were before they got there. How much easier to write expressively about people and places you can touch and meet, like Mrs Young down the road, who can remember 'when the Zeppelin came over in the First World War and made all the door knockers go knock-knock-knock down the street'. Transcribe Mrs Young, be Mrs Young, have a Mrs Young fantasy of where I, (Mrs Young), would most like to be... etc etc.

In all the writing situations I have described, the free verse, oral writing method allows for the easiest expression of idea and feeling. Let Grendel's mother be in the oral mode, let Mrs Young be oral. It is an aspect of *their* 'reality' that the children can best get hold of and re-create. And if you're dealing with ordinary people's history, then children's ordinary everyday language will do just fine to express those people's feelings. Which is the more authentic statement about a nineteenth century house servant; 'Cook gets up at five thirty, lays the fire, empties the ashes, lights the fire... etc.' or 'First thing I have to do, is do the fire, and I hate this because my back is killing me these days...'?

iv The Object Stimulus

This is perhaps the most over-used starting point of all. For example we bring in a skull — describe a skull, encourage metaphorical writing: 'eyes like black stones' etc, look for evocative words and so on.

I think this sort of thing is of very limited value. It often produces formula writing full of 'Beautiful Phrases' and 'Powerful Metaphors' but doesn't have very much to do with any real felt experience.

On the other hand a skull may very well spark off memories of felt experience: Uncle Jeff dying of lung cancer, why cemeteries are such lonely places, where-I'm-going-when-I'm-dead fantasy. This sort of stuff is worth writing down: the voiced thoughts and anecdotes that arise from the stimulus.

It's back to the business of what are children experts in? There's this strange idea that a 'beautiful description' is a Great Poem but an anecdote about Uncle Jeff won't be so great. We think children need to acquire empirical knowledge, so we go about asking them to describe things. But the very moment we ask them to describe, we say 'Good Description' goes like this: metaphor, simile, evocative word. In fact the anecdote about Uncle Jeff is as good a poem about a skull as 'eyes like black stones'.

I feel we should use the stimulus method only if it is as a route into all the kinds of tangential talk and thought. Of course, some people will want just to describe the object, and good luck to them, but if you make the situation as open-ended as I have suggested, then a lot of other possibilities of real felt experience being expressed will arise. After all, the poem about 'closely observed objects' is quite a recent and quite a small part of the total cultural world of poetry, and yet it has almost become the main contemporary poetic form.

I'd make similar observations about the 'Visit stimulus', where a class of kids is taken to look at The River, or The Dump and write a poem about it. It's the 'about it' that is the problem. Of course let's take them anywhere, but 'The River' might, after talk and discussion, spark off thoughts about underwater treasure, the night the tank burst or whatever. It doesn't have to be 'weeds like green fingers caress the bubbles...'

And anyway somebody, (perhaps teacher) could have a whale of a time writing down what everyone says on the way there, while they're there and on the way back: 'my new shoes', 'brother's birthday party', 'my dog', 'wouldn't it be nice to swim in it.' 'I can't swim', 'keep up, George'...

v Drama and Improvisations

Like anecdote telling, drama and impros are an ideal route into Oral Writing because the process is already in the oral mode (apart from mime!) How and when drama arises in schools, varies enormously and drama teachers have many differing views about what drama is for. However, at any point in drama, either to feed *into* the enactment or to take *from* it, it's possible to do some writing: monologues, dialogues, transcriptions of impros, stream-of-consciousness thought-process behind a character's motivation, ritualistic curses, oaths, ceremonies, narrative songs and chants, Greek chorus commentaries etc etc.

The ideal forms for these may be free verse; it may be forms based on traditional forms the children already possess (playground rhymes or pop songs) or it may be something they invent.

It's a sad feature of schooling, especially in secondary schools, where English and Drama are separate, that children can one moment be in a highly expressive, highly fluent frame of mind (in a drama impro) and the next, be tonguetied, helpless, wrong and a 'failure' (in writing a poem). The two activities ideally complement each other.

vi From Story

When stories work, when they really engage the audience, there are obviously many starting points for writing out of them: re-tellings, re-tellings from different points of view, writing scenes that are implied by the narrative but not actually narrated eg: 'what did Goldilocks tell her mum when she got home?' 'what do Rosencrantz and Guildenstern talk about on board the boat to England?' What interests me in the context of this book, is how can a story be a starting point for Oral Writing? This means thinking about monologues, dialogues, voiced thoughts and the like. This means changing the emphasis from reproducing the writer's narrative style to getting inside a character or characters and making them speak.

Again, drama is an ideal route to this but not the only one. Similarly, the *told* story rather than the *read* one is already in an oral mode and so sets up the possibility of oral mode writing.

vii From a Poem

In English teaching today, this is the most common starting point for writing. 'Look — class, here is a poem about sleep, now you write a poem about sleep.' There are two dangers with this method: 1) The child writes not from felt experience but according to expected formulae. 2) The poem is too hard a form to copy and so many children sense failure. These consequences are not inevitable and of course how else will children get a chance to discover different forms if they don't read poems and try writing like that? And after all, educational bookshops are weighed down with books of poems with 'Now you can write a poem like that' written underneath it. However, at the end of the day, the best thing to do with a poem is read it. If the idea of a poem in a classroom is something you do when it's time to write, it starts to negate the reason why we folks write poems in the first place. 'Now children, I want you to read this poem ...' 'Oh no this is where we have to do some writing!' So perhaps the best time to read poems is when the kids know they can't be asked to do some writing, just before playtime or at the end of school. However, that said, either form or content or both in form or content, children *are* alerted by possibilities that reading poems provide, eg: 'I could write *about* that' or 'I could write *like* that'. But, here is a plea from a writer of poems, at least let the route go like this:

READ POEM → DISCUSSION →→WRITE A POEM
                          ↑
              WAIT AT LEAST A DAY!

If this book serves any purpose, it is to say that this route of read-poem to written-poem is by no means the *only* route or necessarily the *best* route. And more than that: if you're interested in Oral Writing, then the chances are your starting points won't be a read-poem *either* because there isn't much Oral Writing Poetry about, or because the activity is too much in the written sphere. You need to get people *talking* to remind them that *what you say,* and *the constructions you use in speech* are OK for putting down on the page.

viii From a Theme

The word 'theme' in fact covers many different approaches. So it might refer to a feeling, an activity, a view of the world, a subject for discussion, and so on. As any teacher knows, this, like the poetry-teaching book, is a favourite of the school text-book approach: a list of 'themes' a variety of kinds of writing within the themes, followed up by exercises. Basically this format has been in operation for the last fifty or sixty years in schools, with the only improvement being in what the textbook writers think is 'good literature'. Perhaps, *some* of the activities suggested have improved too. However, it is what a class unconsciously or consciously perceives happening in the reality of that day, that week, or that term that really matters. It's a bit like the difference between a live performance and a film. We know, in a live performance that it is going on now. And, especially in a live performance that varies with each audience, eg: by having people participate, we know that we are part of that reality, and *can affect it*. In face of a film we can't affect the object itself. Obviously by yelling out 'BOO', in the middle of a slushy bit, we can make the audience laugh, but that is because they know it won't affect the course of the film. Similarly, faced with the immutable themes of the text book, they don't appear to arise out of the lived day-to-day experiences of the kids in that class at that moment. They may do, if it's worked for, if they are threaded into that reality by very careful choosing. But if the theme is plucked for no better reason than it is on page 23 and we were on page 22 yesterday then there is little purpose in the exercise.

So, as in the case of anecdote-child-based, and event-based starting points, I put in the plea that the thematic approach starts out from what you, the teacher, perceives is going on with the children in front of you. Of course, we know that all children, say, 'get angry', so if you start out to talk about anger you'll get somewhere. When I run workshops, this is how I have to begin. I have to start with generalised possibilities where I know I will overlap in some way with everybody's experience before I get down to specifics. But if you're a class teacher then you don't have to deal with the universally applicable. You can be as specific as the kids in front of you, because you know them.

On pages 15-18, I listed a set of themes that might be regarded as constituting an idea of a child's culture. Some of these 'themes' are already shaped in cultural forms like 'songs we know' but others are of a more psychological kind such as 'my fears'. The mix up is deliberate because we need to look at children in that cultural continuum. The problem for the application of this list in the concrete reality of a class of children doing some Oral Writing is that quite a few of them are abstract, like 'my fears'. Any of us can imagine asking a class to write on the theme of 'my fears' and getting a pile of boring rubbish. What we have to do is break 'my fears' down into the specifics of 1) *a moment* 2) *a place* 3) *a time* 4) *a person*. We have to get a child, or children to that place, moment or person, and get them talking about it. Perhaps in the present tense: 'I am standing in the toilet and there's a spider on the wall...' so that 'my fear' becomes a concrete reality.

In the back of our brain, we may have the Theme: 'Fear' coming up in big lights, the important thing with Oral Writing is to keep it out of sight. No child under ten, that I know, would, in a tale about seeing a spider in the loo, naturally come up with the phrase 'my fear' and there's no reason why they should. But as we know, plenty of other expressions of fear would, from 'scary' to 'YAAAAAAAAAAAAAAAAAAA'. All good stuff for Oral Writing.

So to sum up: the key issue with the thematic approach is how to find ways to break down 'The Theme' into the child specific, the time specific, the place specific and the person specific. In the event of our being interested in Oral Writing then we also have to make sure that that specific is dealt with orally, through discussion, taping, monologuing, drama improvisations or whatever, before we get writing. In this way, it's not so much whether we can find the perfect theme for all children we'll ever teach, (thereby making lesson preparation a pushover from here on!) but rather that *any* theme might or might not be the perfect theme dependent on how we make it *specific*.

To illustrate all this, I'll give an example of how I might work with the theme 'Being Ill'. Here's a 'pushover' theme in the sense that every child sitting in front of me has been ill at some time or another. So, surely all I have to say is, 'write about being ill', and they'll write. The poor ones will write very little, the good ones will write a lot but everyone will write something. I think we have to do something else. So I start by asking the children to tell me the names of illnesses they've had, and what kinds of symptoms they've had; Chicken pox, and flu and sneezing and being sick and all that goes up on the board. (In my situation, as a visitor for one hour, I have to be 'chalk-and-talk'). Then I say I want you to imagine (why not do drama here?) being ill now. 'I am ill...' And I say

1 *what can you see?*
2 *what can you hear?*
3 *what can you feel?*
4 *what can you hear people saying?*
5 *what are you saying?*
6 *what are you thinking about?*
7 *what are you daydreaming about?*
8 *what are your what-ifs?*

I say to the children they can write answers to *all* those questions, or *some* of them in any order. The children give answers to the questions with things like: 'mum pouring out the medicine', 'an aeroplane crossing the window', 'the video on downstairs'. So I might write these up on the board, in lines, free verse, the things that the children have said. And they're not 'sentences'. So we construct a writing that is not made out of sentences, but out of individual lines that the children have said. 'But this isn't "writing how you say things"', I hear you cry. No, not in its overall text, but the point is it is *constructed out of oral structures,* oral building blocks. (See 'Irritating sayings' in appendix II page 138)

Through focussing on the specific illness, the specific sense data of that illness, putting it in the present tense and showing the possibility of making a poem out of the list of the sense data — the children are shown the possibility of making the list a narrative, a stream of consciousness, or a cumulative statement or whatever. They can use their voice throughout. So we didn't use a 'Being-ill Poem' as an example; we've freed the children from the 'tyranny of the sentence' and we've got them keyed into the idea that you can write about past events as *if you are there now*...

Another way to look at 'themes' in the area of Oral Writing, is to go from the orally-based theme in the first place. I am thinking of things like:

'You're nagging your mum for something'
'There's a row at the tea table'
'You're playing a game and someone's cheating'
'Your dad promises you something but breaks his promise'
'You get told off?'
'There's an argument over the TV'
'There's a kid over the park and he's trying to rough you up'
'You're being teased'
'Your gran meets you at the door'
'Your mum asks you to tidy your room'
'You tell a lie'

Choosing these themes means thinking about children, thinking about their points of view on life, thinking about their development, thinking about their obsessions.

It means being less worried about 'writing development', or 'introducing them to great literature' or 'making sure that every word is correctly spelt and every construction is grammatical'. It means accepting childishness as authentic, and expressing the authentically childish is a mature thing to do.

Here are a few more 'oral-based' themes:

boasting
bragging you can do things but then you can't
parental warnings

arguments about how to start a game
parents arguing
school dinner chat
what I think the teachers talk about in the staff room
what I overheard my parents saying when I shouldn't
have
verbal fluffs, (mistakes, bloomers, malapropisms,
spoonerisms etc)
looking after younger brothers and sisters
a babysitter looks after you
embarrassing things I have said
parental commands
what bullies say

Group poems like 'irritating sayings' can be constructed
out of one-liners of many kinds: what aunties and grannies
say to you when you first meet them, what shopkeepers
say to your mum when you go with her to the shops, what
people say to each other when they say goodbye and so on.

ix Slang, Dialect and Mother Tongues

Preamble
If there's one topic to raise the hackles of the popular
press, and the hyper-correct school of thought, it's the
sanctity of the prestige dialect, standard English. As it
happens no one can quite agree what standard English *is*
but an awful lot of people are quite sure what it *isn't,* and
go round complaining about Americanisms, split infini-
tives, double negatives, dropped aitches, or whatever.

The main way in which children of 'parents-who-
trained-for-work-orally' fail is in the process of being initiated into written mode writing. Most 'people-who-train-
for-work-orally' speak slang, dialects and/or another language. We can say that the oral is constantly being desig-
nated as 'wrong', 'incorrect', 'common' and generally
undesirable. Cockneys are told in schools not to say

(except in inverted commas), 'I ain't got none'; 'we was laughing', 'youse lot', 'I never done it, honest, sir' and so on. Obviously, the business of what we say and how we say — it is not simply a matter of smartness or cleanliness. What and how we say things is part of a whole social and psychological scene. Labelling what people *say* and how as 'wrong', 'out of order' and 'undesirable' is also labelling *individuals* and *social groups* as 'wrong', 'out of order' and 'undesirable'. The argument against this, is that schools teach standard English so that 'working class kids' get access to 'higher knowledge' and better jobs.

In reply:

Firstly, schools cannot give *all* 'working class kids' (by any definition of the phrase) access to 'better jobs', because they are part of the process that ensures that working class kids get working class jobs. (See 'Learning to Labour' Paul Willis.) Effective social mobility (again by any definition you like) is minimal and what there is can nearly always be traced to out-of-school influences and ambitions.

Secondly, teachers don't change the way people speak. Talking is a social activity. It has to perform its tasks in a social situation or not at all. (Not many people spend much time talking to the wall.) The social situation is the determiner of the way of talking. Of course, the classroom is a social situation but it is such a small one, and one which is dominated by a power relationship between teacher and taught: 'Don't you dare talk to me like that again!' 'Why should I want to speak like the foreman?' might be the reactions of some older school students.

Thirdly, it is true that most theoretical knowledge is written in standard English. But aside from the fact that some isn't, eg: Maths, there are vast areas of knowledge that have nothing to do with standard English, eg: any physically expressive act, dance, pottery, music, sport, design, craft and the like. There is no reason, other than a bad one why we should accept a hierarchy of knowledge where the potter supposedly knows less than the sociologist. Standard English, theoretical knowledge is not 'higher knowledge'. Nor can it be claimed that by providing 'working class kids' with access to standard-English theoretical knowledge, this somehow enables them to 'deconstruct ruling class mystification' (ie: suss who's putting one over on them) as has been claimed. It's activities like organisation, or looking at the structures of the institutions we live in, that may help in this process. Anyway, it is doubtful if any teacher can 'demystify' very much for any pupil because teachers play a dominating role in the mystifying institution the pupils are in.

A whole range of skills that are vital to all of us depend on oral guidance, a slow accumulation of experience, intuition, and inter-personal awarenesses. For example, any of the trades; carpentry, plastering, plumbing and the like; nursing, midwifery, social work and of course teaching itself. It just so happens that our society puts very fixed status on these jobs so the whole argument about teaching children standard English has to be seen in that light. What people are, in effect, saying is that standard English is linked to high and middle status jobs. For teachers to say this, is a kind of vanity: 'Talk like me and you'll get a job like me'. As we know, many school leavers reject this proposition, some because they can't help it, others because they regard a job as a garage mechanic or a market stall-holder preferable anyway. In fact, this business of 'Standard English' is not much more than a means by which the sheep can be separated from the goats — mostly confirming and repeating the separation of the parents into those trained orally and those trained with books.

Children who come from homes where standard English is spoken are at a great advantage over children who come from homes where it isn't, simply because the language of 'good' writing in schools is standard English. The advantaged children do not have to do as much translating. This has nothing to do with 'intelligence' but does explain school 'failure'. The point is that educators are not concerned with an objective phenomenon called 'literacy', the word is already defined as 'literate-in-standard'. Otherwise we could all take exams in 'literacy-in-dialect'.

'Oh but no one will understand you,' cry the educators. However isn't it amazing that Kenny Dalglish, who has one of the strongest Glaswegian mutters I have ever heard, can manage to organise eleven football players from all parts of the UK to be a great football team? Isn't it amazing that two world wars were fought with conscripts from all over the UK mixing and making themselves understood? Isn't it amazing that every year, at trade union conferences delegates from all over the UK meet and discuss theory and practice, in dialect? How do any of them possibly manage? And then isn't it amazing that children in Glasgow learn black New York rapping? And children in Ipswich learn Jamaican dialect through Bob Marley. As many a local newspaper columnist has tried, the bible, Shakespeare, the news, anything can be cast in dialect if we want. And as any E2L teacher knows, literacy in your own dialect was never an obstacle for being literate in anything else.

Practical
So what might be the role of mother tongues (other than English) in Oral Writing? I have worked with Bengali (to be accurate, Sylheti) children in Whitechapel, London. We have talked about arguments with brother and sisters, mums and dads getting cross or whatever. Sometimes we might want to cast that into English but I have made efforts to include legitimate Sylheti phrases in the dialogues. But how to transcribe them? The children might be too young to know Bengali script and anyway they don't speak Bengali, they speak Sylheti. So I get them to *say it out,* and I write phonetically: Brother calls brother 'Black Monkey'; what is it in Bengali? (they call it that) 'Khalla bandor'. All the children in the class can read this and say it. We have a laugh, things feel good. If we're lucky

64

enough to have a Bengali teacher in, she can transcribe it into Bengali script, as well. More laughs. To draw any child's attention to dialect, slang and mother tongue draws attention to the oral. If we do it in a positive way, humbly, eager to learn, interested in what you, the child, come up with; helping to think up ways of representing what you say on the page, then once again, we're not in a situation where we're worrying about whether 'they've got too little to write'. We can suggest pupils write dialogues in dialect with glossaries, translations of serious announcements into dialect; trying to write other people's dialects; dialogues between different dialects; contrasts between thick dialect 'like my dad speaks at work' and not-so-thick. As many of us know, children are often very good at mimicking. We can say to children struggling with standard English constructions in their 'essays', 'stories' or whatever, 'think posh' (if that's the word the kids use to mean 'standard') 'and write like a posh person would say it? Think of a posh person you know and *write* it as if they're *saying* it.' The same kid, who in a drama lesson plays a king, or the president and does it in a standard accent with 99% 'correct' constructions, sits down and can't stop him/herself from writing dialect constructions. *It's because the vital connection between writing and talking has not been made.* When we talk about getting children to write standard, we can say, 'think BBC News', 'think posh', 'think me'. 'Act it onto the page'. I've been amazed at how it has helped London-born Caribbean kids who leave in occasional Caribbean verb agreements or spellings: 'yesterday, he *holl* a cricket ball'. (holl = held). I've found that one of the most useful ways to get talk and writing going about dialect and mother tongues is by bringing into the classroom examples of what can be done on the page. Once again, many pupils know that dialect exists as 'this stuff we're saying' but don't know that it *can* be written down. Of course once you get the thing going in school, then you can build up your own library of examples and don't have to go to books like this!

3. STARTING POINTS (TECHNIQUE)

i Group Poems

In order to alert a class to the fact that what they, as children, say and do is the valid stuff of writing, I might do a group poem with them (see page 97). I might take a chorus line like:

'After dark, after dark'
or
'That's what mum says'
or
'I'm ill, I'm ill'.

Then I might ask each child to offer up one line, one statement, one thing that somebody says. As they say their lines, I write them up on the blackboard, putting in the chorus, every three lines or so. I try to get everybody to offer something and then we say the whole poem together. You can offer the class the chance to copy it word for word, change it how they want, copy it out and then cut it up and rearrange it, start all over again and write their own or maybe take one line from it and expand on it how they want. The end result of all this may be twenty or so poems that would make a nice book around a theme. It's collective, it's individual, it's oral, it's writing, it's something to read. It can sit on the shelves of the class library.

ii The Present Tense

I've already mentioned this in the context of writing the poem about being ill. When we ask children to write about 'what happened on holiday', the writing often comes out wooden, written to safe, easy formulas. One reason is because it's lacking in orality and psychology, ie: 'what people say' and 'what you think'. It seems as if the convention of the formal past tense can act as an inhibitor too.

I sometimes get kids to experiment with the present tense. Let's say they have already written it in the past tense: 'My dad was driving the car...'

I suggest putting it in the present: 'My dad's driving the car ...' to see if it releases more immediate emotions, dialogues and moments. With 'The Magpie and Vitamins' story, I might have asked that child to put herself in the present tense at various points, eg: when she's holding the bird, when she sees the bird is dead, when they're having the funeral and so on. We can ask the sense-data questions on page 59.

Now, as it happens, anyone who listens to how we tell jokes and anecdotes in our daily life, knows that very often we hop to and fro with our tenses. When it comes to good bits or dramatic bits, we bring it into the so-called 'historical present tense'.

'So he says to me...'

'Next thing, this dog comes round the corner...'

We like it, it feels good. Let's get kids writing like that. It helps them get back to what the moment felt like, actually at that moment.

iii Interviews

In the 'Process method' of helping children write, quite a lot of effort is put into 'conferencing', where the teacher discusses the child's writing with the child. The disadvantage, as I have observed it, is that it involves the child making revisions to fit adult preconceptions about correctness: 'Don't write "we", write "My daddy and I"' and the like.

I'm very interested in the idea of sitting down with children and helping them write. I try the interview method.

Let's say we're writing about a dog that ran away.
I say, tell me about it.
She says, we've got a dog called Rex
I write, 'we've got a dog called Rex'

67

and she says, one day he ran away
I write, 'one day he ran away'.
I say, what did you say, when he ran away?
She says, I went mad
I write, 'I went mad'.
I say, but what did you say?
She says, I screamed at my dad.
I said Rex has gone again
I write, 'I screamed at my dad,
Rex has gone again'.
I say, what did he say?
She says, That bloody dog.
You look for it, he's yours
I write,
'dad said,
That bloody dog
You look for it
It's yours'.
I say, did you?
She says, yes
I say, what shall I write?
She says, so I had to go look for it
I write, 'so I had to go look for it'.
I say, did you find it?
She says, yes
I say, what shall we write?
She says, I found him near Olly's
I write, 'I found him near Olly's'.
I say, what's Olly's?
She says, snack bar place
I say, shall I write that?
She says no
I say, so that people will know?
She says no
We've written:
'we've got a dog called Rex
one day he ran away
I went mad

I screamed at my dad
Rex has gone again
dad said that bloody dog
you look for it
It's yours
so I had to go look for it
I found him near Olly's'.

Now we can discuss whether to write about what she thought when she found Rex, or what she said, or what dad said when she came back with Rex, to give us

'I kissed him
and he looked all happy and frisky an' that.
dad said
That bloody dog
more trouble than it's worth.'

I try to write down what the child actually says, I try to get her to focus on the things that people say, and what she actually thinks. Where there are things I don't know or understand I sometimes ask for clarification and then ask if she wants that put down. If it's peer group knowledge, the child might think that there's no reason to put it down because it would make it sound 'un-cool'. On the other hand without the added detail, the story might be incomprehensible to almost everyone. It can be discussed.

You can then hand the child what you've written and he or she can copy, change, or junk, re-set into the present tense, or whatever.

iv Inner Speech, Stream of Consciousness

It is impossible to describe the thought process as a whole. There appear to be conscious and unconscious elements; verbal and not so verbal and non-verbal and how all these mix up and get stuck together is really anybody's guess.

The phrase 'inner speech' is a way to describe *some* of the verbal and conscious thoughts we have: things like, debates with ourselves, questions we meant to ask but never did, the bits and pieces of ideas that float in and out.

In various books on writing, inner speech is described as a kind of *pre*-writing phase. It's what we do *before* the pen hits the page or 'as we do our first doodlings'. This may well be the case, but as it happens, I'm rather fond of my inner speech and I'm all for getting kids to try and reproduce the feel of their inner speech on the page. After all, didn't James Joyce and Samuel Beckett write pretty successful books like that? Consider the idea of Being Lost. Most kids have experienced being lost in a supermarket when they were three or four — running around the corner and then losing mum and dad. Under normal classroom conditions, we might ask a child to write about this memory. Unless directed otherwise, you can bet your best boots that he or she will write it after the style of the 'Magpie and the Vitamins'... 'when I was four, I once etc etc'.

I sometimes suggest another approach. I say to the child, you are lost, present tense. You are there now. What thoughts jump into your head? Ask the sense data questions... the answers may start coming out non-syntactically

— help
— people's legs
— music

Poems that came out of writing this way are on Page 119.

Writing like this has several unspoken messages for children.

1. Inner Speech is OK. Let's hear it.
2. You don't have to write in sentences to be understood or effective.
3. Do you sometimes wonder how your brain works? Maybe the way you've just written represents that.

4. It is possible to write in such a way that how you write means what you write. I'll explain what I mean by this in the next section.

Another way into this stream of consciousness/inner speech writing is to show pupils how you can take a piece of writing, put it into the present tense, and drop the 'thes' and 'as' and anything that slows it up. Turn it into a piece of stream of consciousness writing in front of them and see whether they can then write like that. Another way is to get them to try writing both ways and see which one they like the best.

Getting lost is ideal for this but there are plenty of other ideas:
diving off the top board
facing your dad just after you've done the worst thing in your life
the middle of a nightmare
the process of remembering a nice moment of a holiday
a car crash
the thoughts that come to you when looking at the sky or listening to a piece of music
what you feel like the day before a big day like Eid, or a birthday

v Sensual Writing

This is one of the ways people like to define poetry; making words sound like the thing you're talking about. (Enter onomatopoeia and alliteration.) The process of trying this and doing it is not part of Oral Writing. People doing it do not, by and large, end up with constructions of words that correspond to things we hear people say. This is not to say I am in any way knocking it, or think that it isn't something we should try to do with children. Quite the opposite. I think it's a great thing to try and do because it involves ways of re-expressing experience. The

71

pitfalls are just the same, though, as any 'technique' approach to poetry. You end up with stuff that sounds great but in essence means very little to whoever wrote it.

However, arising out of a playing with words session, or from a piece of stream of consciousness writing, it might seem right to have a go at this kind of poetry writing.

You can show children that in order to say that it's raining quite a lot you can use any of the following:

You can say;
    'It's raining'
    'It's raining cats and dogs'
    'it's raining a lot'
    'wow it's raining!'
    'boy is it raining.'
    'it's really coming down out there'
    or
    'rain-raining
    rain-raining
    rain-raining
    rain-raining'

You might want to say that you saw a snake so you can say;
    'I saw a snake'
    'look out there's a snake' 'YAAAAAAA, SNAKE!'
    'A snake was lying in the grass'
    or
    'slinking, slithering, sliding, snake'

You might want to say;
    'yesterday I went running'
    'I was running'
or
    'foot
    down
    breath

foot
up
breath
up
breath
down
up
down
breath
up
down
up
down
breath'

It is beyond the scope of this book to spend much time on this matter. The problem about it as a way of working in schools is that quite often children ask us 'what's the point?' And given that the writing and reading of poetry should be fascinating, enjoyable, intriguing and all that, then if the person trying it doesn't see the point of doing it then neither can I. For me it's a nice game to play, sometimes it seems a right way to talk about something so that people understand what I'm trying to say. On the other hand an awful lot of writing like this can sound like a load of old pretentious phooey. It can simply be a way of taking away the immediacy of the event or feeling and making something just *sound* good. I'm not of the school of thought that thinks that this kind of poetry writing is 'real poetry' and that all the other stuff this book has been about so far, is a kind of *pre*-poetry. Many experts on poetry would disagree with this because they believe poetry is special and separate from 'ordinary language'. It should have 'a diction of its own'. I don't think we should lumber children with such pre-conceptions. We can show them poets who like to write sensually; we can give them opportunities to try it themselves. Then they can take it or leave it.

vi Shape Poems

Just as we can write things that sound like what they
mean we can write things that *look* like what they mean:

On page 75 are some examples by children (seven year
olds):

Once again, this is not Oral Writing. It's something I enjoy
doing and something that many kids enjoy too. I'm not
going to make any great claims for it as a tremendously
valuable activity other than to say that it falls into the category of 'language-as-putty'. In a world where language
does seem to have a power and mystery that only adults
understand, it's quite nice for children to see that they can
muck about with the shapes of letters, the shapes of
words, the shapes of phrases and the shapes of whole
sequences. Some children can and will; others just ain't
bothered. Some find it really funny and can't stop playing,
others don't see the point.

So long as it is something the children enjoy it is valid
because it means they are really *playing* with language,
which is an empowering act. It helps to reverse the dominated feeling many children have about language.

vii Playing With Words

There are several books on the market that cover this
area.

I aM going to cross this Busy road   Stephen

Beep

Screech

Roll Ro ll Roll Roll
oll Roll Roll Roll Roll
R oninons   Sauce   R
R   Hot dog   oll
Roll   Roll   Roll Roll Roll
Roll   Roll   Roll Roll   Roll

happy

sad

The games I've found that children enjoy are:

Making up notices, especially mad ones, and drawing them up full size. As a starting point you can use the word, 'word'.

PLEASE KEEP OFF THE WORDS
PLEASE DO NOT FEED THE WORDS
NO WORD GAMES HERE

and then move on to: laughing, feet, noses, jokes, human beings. Notices to look at:

KEEP LEFT
MIND THE STEP
NO FOOD HERE
NO SMOKING
HOUSE FOR SALE
AT YOUR LOCAL DEALER NOW
BUSINESS AS USUAL

Knock-knocks
Knock-knock jokes for young children involve quite a sophisticated use of language. Collecting and inventing new ones is a good language play. My favourite:

Knock knock
Who's there?
Cows.
Cows who?
No they don't. Cows moo.

Puns
A formula that children use is

'What is the strongest fish?'
'Mussels' (mussels, muscles)

76

We can give them words that'll help them make up new ones. (bore, boar) (boy, buoy) (a rest, arrest) (ewe, you) (knows, nose) (fair, fare)

Football results
   Manchester United 1 Manchester City lost
   Crystal Palace 2 Buckingham Palace 1
   Wolves 8 a cheese roll and had a cup of tea 2
   Aldershot 3 Buffalo Bill shot 2.

I've found that boys between nine and twelve like making up these. Blackpool, Motherwell, West Ham, Bath, Swansea, Burnley, Brighton get them going, but a copy of all four league tables helps.

Guests at the ball
Another everyday game that involves quite sophisticated wordplay.

   Ladies and gentlemen —
   late arrivals at the clothes shop ball:
   Mr and Mrs Rack
   and
   their daughter Anna (Anorak)

   Ladies and gentlemen —
   late arrivals at the chippy's ball:
   Mr and Mrs Atterkechup
   and their son Tom
   (tomato ketchup)

Bacon Slicers
If you slice words up and say them quickly you have a nice sound. It sometimes sounds better if you cheat in the way you pronounce the 'slices'.

Everybody
verybody
erybody
rybody
ybody
body
ody
dy
y

pronounced:

everybody
verybody
erry body
rye-body
why-body
body
oddy
die
why

Try:

calamity — the ending goes better with Mighty, eye-tee, tie, why

catastrophe — ending strophee, trophy, rophy, ophy, phee, hee, ee.

It gives children a chance to play with why letters can represent different sounds.

Shampoo, Friday, difficulty are some more.

Blankety-blank

Those with long memories might be able to remember this being played on TV. What word can you fill in here? Day (blank) eg: daytime, or daydream.

Head (blank); head ache, head case and so on.

You can put the blank at either side of the word or both. Young children tend to put adjectives in, if you put the blank in front — not that this matters!

Other words: time, face, side, right, foot, rock, dog, call, water, cross.

Word bans

What if you banned any word that sounded like 'four', that is: 'four', 'for' and 'fore' and from now on everyone must say 'five'.

'What for?' becomes 'what five?'

'Forget' becomes 'five-get'

'Forefinger' becomes 'fivefinger'

In space, they ban the words, 'sit', 'stand' and 'lie' and now the word 'float' must be used.

'Let sleeping dogs float'.

'Do you underfloat what I am saying?'

'When I come into the room, I want everyone to float up.'

Ban all colours except the colour purple.

Ban and change parts of the body.

viii Simile and Metaphor

It is an extraordinary thing about literary culture that top of the hit parade of 'good writing' goes *metaphorical writing*. What seems to have happened is that the word 'poetry' is being interpreted in many places as meaning 'metaphorical writing'. You write about a process or an object and fill it with a consistent but surprising pile of metaphors and you've got a 'good poem'.

Can metaphors, children and authenticity be mixed? One of the routes I've found useful is to get the kids to record the metaphors in use by kids round them, people at home, grandparents or people on the telly (metaphor to include idiom, simile etc).

'He couldn't punch his way out of a paper bag'
'sick as a parrot'
'he doesn't know his arse from his elbow'
'your eyeballs look like two pissholes in the snow'
'you're a pain in the neck'
'that car really gobbles up the geography'
'well, we're really cooking on the front burners here'

We can collect these over a few weeks, we can write a class poem out of them. We can show how people like Billy Connolly, Bill Cosby, Mike Harding, Jasper Carrott etc, make up new ones. We can make up new ones ourselves. We can perhaps try writing about something using new ones.

In other words, metaphor already exists in the genius of everyday speech. The truly creative process doesn't have to be the thinking up of new esoteric and exciting ones. It can be a way of finding out about our oral tradition, what we already possess and how we can be creative within that tradition, in the way Billy Connolly is. This is as 'poetic' as Gerald Manley Hopkins, only a different sort of 'poetic'.

ix Other Techniques

There are hundreds of books on the market that are full of the techniques of poetry, haikus, limericks, cinquains and how to get kids to do more of the same. I have written this one in order to show that there is another basis for writing: the oral mode. I suggest that on that foundation, kids' interest in many different kinds of writing can be more easily fostered than by the 'technique' approach. However the metaphor(!) 'foundation' does not really fit the bill. I want to indicate that even when these other areas are attempted (metaphorical writing, shape poems, haikus, sensual writing and the like), it is vital that we keep our eyes and ears on the oral tradition. I don't accept that other kinds of writing are superior, more profound, more valuable than the most simple and direct kinds of Oral

Writing. We don't have to accept the 'Great Writers' theory of education. They don't study Siberian lullabies, Aboriginal creation songs, New York raps, Bill Cosby monologues, in University Eng. Lit. departments. Nor do they study what our mums say when they're angry, what it feels like to be seven and have chicken pox, or what babysitters do. We can and it is just as 'Great'.

CHAPTER 4
Publishing and Performing

For writing not to be a rehearsal; for writing to be the real thing, then every writer has to know what it feels like to have a real audience. The teacher alone is not an audience. It is essential for any child writing to get to know what it feels like to have other people, who are not in the teacher-pupil relationship, reacting to what's been written. This completes the chain described in the model on page 35 and the description of writing as 'changing' on page 24.

PUBLISHING

Classrooms could be mini-publishing houses. The act of individual writing and book-making or collective book-making could be going on the whole time. Children can become experts on how to make books interesting and attractive. Their books can sit on the shelves alongside the best of children's literature and be read and re-read many, many times. Experiments with presentation, word processor print-outs, typing, mono-prints, photocopies, duplicating, thermo-stencil, web-offset at the local college can be going on all the time. There is no need for scrappy little exercise books, except to write in rough and for private diaries.

It is in this context, that spelling, punctuation and presentation have a role. The reason why we spell and punctuate is so that Carlton and Aisha can read what we've written. The reason why we lay out work neatly and decorate it, is so that Carlton and Aisha will *want* to read it.

Books in the adult world have to be edited and proof read. Children can be editors and proof readers. That is spelling for a purpose. People in real life, other than teachers, have the job of correcting spelling as a career. Let children do the same.

Of course, books are not the only way to publish things. Schools offer the opportunity to experiment with other forms, wall displays, wall magazines, news sheets, broadside sheets, pamphlets, cards and the like.

Many parents are typists, have access to expensive printing and duplicating machines. Time can be hired on such machines. Parents love to have and buy well-produced magazines full of their children's work. It always amazes me how you can go to one school and these magazines and class books are being churned out all the time and you go to another school and there is nothing. Making books, magazines and the like can pull parents into a process that makes children (and parents too) writers, editors, printers, designers, sales organisers, accountants. Of course it doesn't look like lessons. It doesn't look like 'education', but it is.

Everything that enables schools to involve parents and children in writing is what's right about schools. The effort to overcome obstacles that prevent us from publishing, is part of a wider struggle for emancipation that goes on in the rest of society. That's why it's worth doing. I think one of the most important lessons I learnt at school was the constant effort it was to get a school play and a school magazine off the ground.

PERFORMING

It's ironic and probably quite revealing that though this book is about Oral Writing, it's taken this long to get to the act of performing. The performing has two sides to it: pre- and post-publication. I have already covered the pre- in drama, collecting of oral tradition and improvisations.

The post- needs dwelling on.

It is one odd thing about schools and their relationship with 'high art' that in the real world, theatre is a highly rated art form and yet, in schools, we rarely ask children to write sketches, monologues, and plays that they will perform. Playwriting is a respectable enough art form, isn't it? Writing TV sketches and plays are OK. Why shouldn't schools be places that encourage such an activity? It uses all the literacy, presentation and punctuation skills. Drama teachers often don't have the time to get the kids to transcribe their improvisations — nor necessarily do they think it's that important. Classroom teachers on the other hand are often too busy chaining kids to their seats to take on the problem of getting them *on* their feet improvising. Yet the whole process, in the real world, is rated as 'high art' — master classes at the National Theatre, Peter Brook creates an epic masterpiece.

Improvisations → transcription → adaptation → performance is as great a medium for young people as it is for adults in the theatre.

A lot of discussion takes place in drama teachers' circles about who performance is for. A distinction is made between i) drama where we do it for ourselves: no audience in mind, in order to explore imaginative, psychological, and social themes; and ii) drama that is for show, for assemblies, parents, classmates and audiences. I'm in favour of Oral Writing in both i) and ii).

Schools are tremendous places to experiment with dramatic forms. There is no limit on intimate theatre spaces or places. Theatre can be spectacle, participatory, naturalistic, epic, improvised-every-time, or whatever. Review, cabaret, montage can all be tried. All the kinds of writing I have talked about in this book can find their way back into the totally oral in school performance.

Anecdotes can be acted naturalistically or narrated for assemblies. The narrator can be external to the action or part of it. Kids can experiment with what seems the best. Nonsense poems, sensual writing, stream of consciousness can all be represented in a dramatic form. Just as in schools we should strive to make the presentation of all books be of the highest kind then so we should with drama. I can't describe the emotions that come over me when I work in a school: the children do great Oral Writing and a week or so later they 'read' their pieces in assembly in a low mutter that no one can hear. It virtually defeats the whole purpose of the enterprise. Let them feel and see the collective pleasure there is in performing and watching shows put on by people they know. Schools can not only be publishing houses, they can be community theatres. A few classrooms turning out the oral culture and oral writing of all the children in a class makes enough material to fill hours of theatre time. We have all the facilities for this: typewriters, paints, tape recorders, sound equipment, duplicating machines, slide projectors. Let's do it.

PS. Talking of slide projectors — a great form for kids is the tape slide show. Perform the poems on to tape, take photos of relevant stuff, put the cues on the tape — you've got a show.

CHAPTER 5
What Books?

Is Rosen really suggesting that kids could be producing all this stuff without bringing in hundreds of books? What about great literature?

No. What I have tried to say is that the chaining of the *writing* of poetry to the *reading* of poetry is bad for both. The writing of poetry has to be linked to the oral expression of experience — from an early age, often but not exclusively.

Reading of poetry has to be linked with enjoyment, pleasure, fascination, curiosity and discovery. The relationship between the two needs to be indirect.

What does this say about classroom organisation? It means that there are poetry books lying about in handy places. It means that children have the opportunity to read poems on to tape recorders; have times when they can request and perform favourites. It means that you, as an experienced reader and performer, can slot poems into appropriate moments — in the light of what a child has said, like: 'I hate night-time', or at moments when there is nothing else to do — five minutes before the end of school.

In secondary schools, the great weight of 'comprehension' hangs over the reading of poetry. Many of the questions asked in comprehension tests presuppose answers that are very dubious. If we really want students to 'understand' a poem then who's to say that comprehension is the way? For example, if you ask a group of students to work out what is the best way to perform a poem, what judgments will they bring to bear on the process? Tone, meaning, change of mood, emphasis, and all those things that we folks who write the stuff want our audience to pick up on. It is an activity that represents for me a connection that has to be kept up at all costs: the relationship between the *printed* poem and the way it can be said. This means giving kids the texts of what we read to them. It means performing what they've got in front of them. It does not mean reading in silence and answering academic questions in a vacuum. Long live the photocopier!

But read what?

So long as the connection between what's read and what is to be written is not direct, then I say read anything and everything. Try it and see, I don't accept any of the criteria of 'great poetry', not so great, and not great, because the occasions when we meet the poem can be so different. Who we are and where we are are just as important as 'how good is the poem?' The most important attitude to have to poetry is an irreverent one. Just because someone else says, 'it's great' doesn't mean it *is* great for you or your class. Just because *you* say 'it's great' doesn't mean it's great for *them*. No poetry critic, no 'lit.crit.' expert is ever going to rate Roald Dahl's 'Dirty Beasts' and 'Revolting Rhymes'. But the kids know that they're perfect examples of their own kind. The whole point is that poetry is a matter of 'horses for courses'. What counts is what is appropriate for the moment, for the time, for the mood, for the person, for the occasion. Poetry is not some great immobile slab of beauty that makes you 'great' by looking at it. Every poem enters a certain personal and social dynamic. A critic's dynamic is writing alone in a study away from family and friends. It's him or her and the written word. Teachers' dynamics are not comfortable or solitary. They are: Monday morning, cold day, the classroom; or Saturday night, school journey, just before bedtime; or Friday night, parents evening; Thursday morning assembly; The people are different too — beyond the ken or interest of the critic. The kid who lives in the Salvation

Army home and sits under the table; the kid who has just arrived from a peasant community in the heart of Bangladesh; the madly-in-love-with-George Michael (girl, the Caribbean, the Greek, the Scots, the Travellers' kid. All kids are under the various pressures and influences I have tried to describe earlier: many kids have cultures other than white middle class, academic and literary. If it's poetry that interests us then we have to give the kids the right to have what *they* want just as much as we have what *we* want. Is pop music really all rubbish? No of course it isn't. Can we lay our hands on the lyrics? When I was at Vauxhall Manor school, a record came out called, 'Up Town Top Rankin' which was sung in Caribbean dialect. I photocopied three hundred copies of the words; stood on the corridor and handed them out. They were gone in twenty minutes. One of the cleverest pieces of literature I have ever heard was written and performed by a guy called Smiley Culture. It was called 'Cockney Translation' and it involved him singing at breakneck speed, Caribbean and Cockney dialect phrases: 'Cockney calls him "The Law" we call him "Babylon".'

When you bought the record, it had the words printed with it.

'Your Own Stuff Press' in Nottingham has printed dialect poems by an ex-miner called Barry Heath. They're about his childhood. They're in free verse. Occasionally the record world throws up musicians who write story songs and ballads. (Dylan, Springsteen, Simon, and Country and Western.) When they're good they're as good as anything. There's one reason why they may make better sense for children: they're written in the idiom that they live with.

So when I say 'read anything and everything' that does-n't mean Donne AND Eliot AND Hughes. It means Donne, Eliot, Hughes, Lennon, Marley, Chuck Berry, Smiley Culture, Chas and Dave, and the genius Anon. Basically, the stuff you need is not in anthologies. Make your own anthologies, it won't cost you anything except the photocopying paper. Long live the loose leaf ring binder! And in my list of poets have to go the kids who are in front of you. Their books and broadsides, and posters or whatever can sit alongside the other books.

Just on this matter of reading — which frequently gets reduced to a skill — surely one of the most interesting things to read is what a friend of yours has just written. You might even make an effort to read it — more of an effort than you'd made to read 'Bob And His Dog', or 'Bill on the Hill'. Kids reading each others' books is reading. There are not two processes 1) 'learning to read' and 2) 'reading', so what you read might as well be *worth* reading. Otherwise why bother? You can't expect children who go home and switch channels for themselves to have to take seriously the idea of reading something that bores them stiff just because it's good for them. It's hard enough to get them to drink medicine.

I've found that schools that have got right this business of finding things for kids to read use a combination of all of the following. Note 'all', ie: they attack from all sides.

1   Regular book-making, magazine making, wall displays by the children. Books accessible at all times.
2   A good supply of books in the classroom, changed at regular intervals.
3   A regular parent-child-teacher run bookshop.
4   Use of the local educational authority's resource library to support class work.
5   Use of the local library, local archive and the local history staff.
6   Have a regular book exchange time when children bring in books they've bought, read, recommended and swap. Allow time for discussion and oral reviewing.
7   Teacher keeps a record of what books every child reads. Children themselves can do this and simply hand in.
8   Having times when the teacher reads introductions,

first chapters and book blurbs to kids. My dad
described how he used to come into a classroom with
a big box of books, start reading the first page of a
book and whoever said 'ME' first got the book, and so
on through the box.

9   Having a parents and teachers scheme where parents
become involved in reading with the kids, to the kids,
listening to the kids reading, buying books from the
school bookshop and so on.

10   Organising a classroom so that a variety of ways of
reading are possible: being read to by a teacher, being
heard reading by a teacher or parent or helper, kids
reading to each other, kids reading on to tape
recorders.

11   Burn 'Bob and his Dog' and 'Bill on the Hill'.

If this book does nothing else but suggest to one teacher
somewhere that it's worth trying to implement all eleven
of this list then I'll die a happy man. One of the most dis-
tressing things in my life has been to stand in my son's
classroom on several occasions throughout the school year
and see the same tatty pile of books heaped up in the corner next to where Michael and Joe used to fight.

APPENDIX I
Don't Pull up Your Trouser Legs
Before You See the Sea

YOUNG PEOPLE, CULTURE AND THE SCHOOL

The word 'culture' is used, misused, abused at least a million times a week. I am not going to try some new and ultimate defining stunt that bottles up the word once and for all. I want to use the word in its loosest, vaguest way, namely to mean 'the way people carry out their affairs together'. What interests me is young people's culture, how this is expressed and how schools react to it.

Any given cultural form, whether it be a poem, a slang word, a garment, a dance or whatever, can be found to originate from one or more of three groups:

1   me and my family group;
2   me and my social or peer group;
3   me and my national, or cultural, or ethnic, or class group (depending on how I choose to define myself or how others choose to define me).

Consider the following: four black fourteen-year-old boys get together in a classroom after school with two tape recorders. On one tape recorder a dub version of a Sugar Minott track plays, on the other a blank tape records the dub track and whatever the four boys have to say. They spend the next half hour 'toasting'. This is an oral technique, part improvisational poetry performed by Jamaican and Black British DJs which has grown up in Jamaica and in Britain. It has now become not merely a means of intro-

91

ducing tracks to dance to, but a form in its own right, with international stars like Yellowman, 'Clint Eastwood' and many others.

Here is an extract of what the boys did:

Danny   Here dem style now
Dem talk 'bout me brown jaja
and no how me black
me get up every morning
me run round the track
me inna track suit
anna shorta bobbysocks
but me atta me atta me no wanna borrow datta
me atta, me atta me no wan no more a datta
Winston, I beg yah come inna dis
ribbitta mashitta garatta
lettissa saladda oniona
melanna whatitta gettitta lanitta

Winston   Here no style
Inna O inna O Titan inna O
Inna O inna O Titan inna O
Say go say Titan bum go on de go
Say no DJ coulda touch me any'ow
Me hotta dan de sun in de Colorado
Me cooler dan de breeze dat de west wind blow
Inna O inna O reek it up and rock it so
Caw when I was a yout me father wan name me Joe
Me father said yes and me mother said No
Bom go say go Tippa Titan on de go
Bom go say go Tippa Titan on de go
Caw inna sweety shop I said dem have Polo
Dem have Marshmallow also Rolo
Dem a chat bout fe gi' your girl your last

Polo
Say no DJ coulda touch me' any'ow
Me fav'rite programme thatta Hawaii-Five-0
Caw when dey show it me jussa mek de music flow
Bom go say go Tippa Titan on de go.

I have no idea how much of this is totally original or how much is part quoted from other DJs, except that the whole act is totally free-wheeling and improvised. No print, no paper, no writing. It obviously has origins in group 3, as it is a piece of ethnic group culture. By doing it together it becomes 2 — peer group culture to be made and shared. *Some,* though not all, has origins in personal home experience, so is in category 1 (especially as the form enables the DJ to boast, taunt and produce amazing revelations about his personal life or other people's). In other words, as a cultural form for these four boys it is situated right in the heart of their lives.

I think when this occurs the importance of the activity is very special. They are making and producing something that has reverberations through all three major spheres of their identity. Now let us ask The Beastly Question. What is the schools' response to this activity? A combination of ignorance, indifference, contempt or hostility. In other words, a huge mismatch takes place between boys like these and the school. Let it be said, this was not the case at the school where this went on.

Now, I would suggest it would be useful to look at any number of cultural forms that children use, and apply the same method. But which ones? And how might we describe the total 'Culture' of a young person or group of young people? How can we do it so as to include the oral diversity, the wealth of personal experience and the network of abstract ideas and opinions? One way of getting to such a description would be to consider the components of any young persons' culture: For list see pages 15-18.

Many of these components are totally different in kind and many overlap with each other or can be mixed; for example, 'Promises' and 'Family'. The list is intended to be useful and is not watertight. Also, an approach to any one of them can involve an individual, an individual's description of somebody else or a group. The list has grown out of working with all ages of children and school-children. Mostly, this has been in an informal way in corners of classrooms, libraries and corridors, often nudging alienated people into writing down or taping scraps of their identity.

Given the space it would be possible to illustrate each one of these categories with an example of how they might be expressed. For instance, a piece of writing, a tape slide show, a tape, a piece of improvised drama, a song or a drawing. In each case the example could be any of the following kind: 'creative', reportage, factual, speculative, or transcripts of other people's words.

So let's take some of the categories.

i Proverbs
(From a first-year class in a girls' comprehensive school in East London)

My Mother Always Says...
Tracy Parkes is in 1K. Her mother was born in Jamaica. These are some of her favourite sayings. Tracy has also explained what they mean.
1   You can take a person to the country, but you can't take the country out of him. It means you can't change a person's inborn nature.
2   Show me your company & I'll tell you who you are. It means people tend to mix with others when they have got the same things in common.
3. If you want to know your friend from your enemy, lie on the sidewalk drunk. It means how to find a true friend.

4   a) You never miss the water until the well runs dry.
    b) A cow never knows the value of its tail until called to
    part with it. They mean you never know the true value
    of things until it's too late.

Beyza Beyaztas is in 1K. Her mother was born in Turkey.
Her other ancestors come from Romania and from Greece.
Beyza has written her family sayings in Turkish and then
translated them and told us what they mean.

1.   *Denizi gormeden pacalarina sivama.*

        Before you see the sea, don't pull up your trouser
legs. It means don't do something too soon. For example,
don't get all your holiday clothes ready before you know
where you're going.

2.   *Samanin altindan su yurutme.*

        Don't take water from under the hay. Meaning:
Don't do something without anybody looking, e.g. if you
are getting an apple without your mum looking, she would
turn and say *'Samanin...'*

3.   *Baklavyi azindan cikar.*

        Take the Bakla out of your mouth. Meaning:
Hurry up and say it, as we would say, 'spit it out'. (Bakla
is a sweet.)

ii Special days
(By a fourth-year primary boy in East London, tape transcript.)

In St Lucia there's a festival. There's a thing called D.
Satan, it's all in red and it's got a long white beard and it
looks like the devil. They've got a man all in tar with feathers on — he chucks things at you — like a staff, a pole with
a handle, and things like that.

    It goes all through the streets. There's men that dress
up as women and you can go on to Castris marsh, and in
the square they have a steel band playing and things like
that.

I was there and it's like you're in hell. They chase after you, and if they catch you, they put you in a cart and take you off. Only they don't really take you away, they just dress you up and you come back with them. It's like a procession. The day is called Festival Day.

iii Story told by my dad.
(Tape transcript from the same boy.)

This story is about a dance hall in Dennery, a part of St Lucia and they used to have a song

De devil day tap, tap
De devil day tap, tap
You defraid Satan
Dat Mysteriuss man
He sure can can.

Every time they were singing and dancing this song, the door would open and a creature would come in, half man, half cow with wings.

And so now whenever people hear this song, they turn it off. The people ran out of the hall and the thing just danced round the hall and disappeared.

iv My room
(By a third-year primary boy in East London.)

Mount Wardrobe
On Saturday
I go climbing up on my wardrobe
It takes me half an hour to get up
I climb and climb
The more I climb the tireder I get
Sometimes if we fall off we swim ashore
The shore is the bed
We pretend that the floor is water.
Sometimes I can jump up
from the floor to the wardrobe.

v Local legend

(By a second-year boy in a North London comprehensive.)

One day, ten years ago, where my flats are now there was a factory called Stevens Ink factory and one day one of the foremen was checking up on the machines to see if it was working properly, when suddenly he fell in.

He gave a loud scream, but by the time a worker got there the foreman was dead. He was chopped up into mincemeat.

Now where my flats are, now people say you can sometimes see the foreman scream, then he vanishes.

vi Games

(A group poem by five first-year primary children)

We play police
out in the playground
we run around
out in the playground
we play 'had'
out in the playground
we play jellybeans
out in the playground
we fall over
out in the playground
we play kisschase
out in the playground
we play mummies and daddies
out in the playground
we get told off
out in the playground
we play kick-ups
out in the playground
we found a coat in the bin
out in the playground
we play bingly-bongly
out in the playground

we play emergencies
out in the playground
we play Grange Hill
out in the playground
we play 'Mother may I?'
out in the playground
we play with our friends
out in the playground.

vii How we met
(By a fourth-year boy in a North London Comprehensive.)

I was on the train
going to Loftus Road
to see qpr against Arsenal
On the train I saw this boy
on his own
I went up to him
and said 'Are you going to this match?'
he said, 'Yes.'
So I asked him his name.
He said, 'Frank.'
He asked me what team do I
support,
so I said, 'Arsenal.'
Then he punched me in the face
and ran off.

viii Traditional story
(By a third-year secondary boy of Bengali origin.)

The Crocodile and the Monkey

Over there was a monkey he use (sic) to live in a tree. At the river side in the river there was a crocodile. When the monkey eat the sweet fruits and he use to throw the fruits in the water. The crocodile use to say if I made friends with the monkey then the monkey will give me more fruits.

One day the monkey went to the river to drink water.

The crocodile said, 'My friend monkey, do you like to be my best friend?'

The monkey said, 'OK I will be your friend.'

The monkey use to give the crocodile sweet fruits to eat.

One day, the crocodile decided to eat the monkey. The crocodile thought if he eat the monkey's heart he will find a good taste.

So one day the monkey was crossing the river. In his hand he had a stick. The crocodile came and got the monkey's leg.

The monkey said, 'Stop it crocodile. If you want to eat me, you're holding my stick.'

So the monkey gave his stick to the crocodile and said, 'There's my leg.'

The crocodile got hold of his stick and the monkey swim and he get out of the river and never again went near the river.

ix Traditional rhyme
(First-year girl in a South London comprehensive.)

Mary had a little lamb
she thought it very silly
she threw it up into the air
and caught it by his willy
was a watchdog
sitting on the grass
along came a bumble bee
stung him on the ask
no questions
tell no lies ever seen a chinaman
doing up his flies
are a nuisance
bugs are worse
that is the end of my very silly verse

x A topic on black history
(From a girls' comprehensive in East London.)

Have You always lived in England?

I haven't always lived in England, no, I came here in '69, 1969, no 1959.

Mr...?

Cleary, my name is. Patrick Cleary.

What country did you live in before?

I lived in the island of Curacao, that's in... I'm a Grenadian. But the island of Curacao is different to the island of Grenada.

Why did you come to England?

Why did I come? Hmm. I wanted to travel. I wanted to travel. It's, it's the habit of the people in my island, or in the Caribbean as a whole, to travel. When you come of a certain age, you must want to go abroad. And see what's around.

What do you remember about the first day?

Busy. Speed. The trains and the speed that everyone was moving. I think that that was my first impression.

How old were you?

Nineteen. I was nineteen years old.

You didn't have to answer that one anyway!

What sort of reactions did you get from white people?

What reactions? Curiosity, I think was the main thing. Very curious and ask questions, a lot of questions, I think.

What did you think England was going to be like before you came?

I thought it would be much, mm, much cleaner, and, and umm, look much more prosperous in its appearance, structurally and otherwise.

How do you feel about England now?

Well, I'm earning a living in this island and I feel to survive one has got to work very hard. In every country now you've got to work to survive. So there is not anything particular with England.

Where did you first live when you came to England?

First I lived in Huddersfield; I had some cousins there. And I went to London in 1962, I live in Ealing now. I have lived in Ladbroke Grove, Tooting.

What work did you do when you first came to England?

My first job was in a stamping forge, stamping metal to make forges for different industries. I've worked in engineering. I've been trained as a tailor and continued at college. I'm a master tailor by profession.

Do you prefer living in England or where you were born?

Well, where I was born has changed quite a lot now to when I left. If I can earn a good living and look after my family the way I am doing here, then I would prefer to live there. It depends.

Would you like to go back?

Yes I would. Yes. But I can't say exactly when.

Where do you come from, anyway?

Barbados. And Pakistan.

Are any of your children Rastas?

Well now, explain the real meaning of the term 'Rasta' to me?

xi Kinds of work
(Interview with a fireman on a picket line during the fireman's strike of 1976, carried out by third-year girls from a South London comprehensive.)

What do you think a fireman's basic wage should be?

It should be — what we're asking for — the average male working wage — that's the average of all male people in England who are at work: an average of that plus the government's 10 per cent, which in real terms works out to about £20 a week increase.

How do you think the television are treating your case?

Up till the end of last week we was getting very good TV coverage, as you know. We was on every news bulletin etcetera etcetera and since President Sadat's visit it's not been so good. I think this is primarily because they are taking a direct government line. The government are not directly censoring the newspapers, but they are, how can I put it? directing them not to publish things that it would be politically unsafe for them to publish; i.e. they publish the death figures, the people that get killed but they won't publish how in fact they died and whether they was in direct cause of the strike.

(The girls ask if they are paid while they're on strike and hear that they're not, that they can draw supplementary benefit for wives and children but not for themselves.)

How do you pay for rent and all that?

The rent? Unfortunately as from December 1st the rent goes out the window. If you're in rented accommodation, the Social Security will make sure you won't lose your tenancy. If you're like me, a mortgage holder, then you've got to make arrangements with your mortgage company to suspend one month's payment of your mortgage.

Do you prefer not doing anything at all instead of going and stopping a fire?

No, of course not. All firemen have got a sense of responsibility. They much prefer to be putting out people's fires and helping the public, which is what they do all the year round, anyway, than standing out here on the picket line getting freezing cold and not getting paid for it. Unfortunately, it comes to this situation where a fireman's pay and conditions were getting so far behind everybody else that the men are leaving the job wholesale for other occupations with more money; and what was left of the union membership decided to take this action to illustrate it to the public and to obtain more money.

xii Songs
(Composed by second-year girls in a comprehensive school.)

Joanne's eyes are so big
Bird's eyes, bird's eyes
Just as big as fifty pence pieces
Bird's eyes, bird's eyes
And when she comes around the corner
Bird's eyes, bird's eyes
Her eyes always come first
Whose eyes? Her eyes? ah those eyes
Bird's eyes, bird's eyes.

xiii Traditional rhyme
(By a first-year boy at an East London comprehensive.)

Oh where is my smokey
all covered in sand
I killed a Leeds united supporter
with an elastic band
I went to his funeral
I went to his grave
The vicar came up to me
and asked me my name
I answer politely
with a bicycle chain
he took me to court for this
and the judge so did say
you will go to Borstal
for a year and one day
me old woman fainted
me old man dropped dead
and me poor little brother
shot the judge in the head
there's bars on the windows
there's bars on the door
and even the pisspot
is chained to the floor

xiv Dialect
(By a second-year girl at a South London comprehensive.)

In trouble
Me and me broda was on we wa from school. Me was 6 then an he was 8. On de way from school me wanted to go tilet. We bote wanted to go in the sweety shop. So we did. While we was sartin out wat we was going fe buy, me wet me self. Dere was a great big puddle on de floor roun abote me. Wen I reach ome me broda tell me muda an she tell me off an tell me sa if me did wan fi go tilet me shoulda go ome straight away an not stop inna sweety shop.

English
I and my brother was on our way from school. I was 6 and he was 8. On the way from school I wanted to go the toilet. We both wanted to go to the sweet shop. So we did. While sorting out what we was going to buy, I wet myself. There was a great big puddle on the floor round about me. When I reached home my brother told my mother and she told me that if I wanted to go to the toilet I should of come straight home and not stop in the sweet shop.

I hope that these pieces, by using some of the categories on my list, will suggest the scope of this approach with young people. I don't want to represent all schools as foully oppressive places BUT... there is a problem in that many schools ignore these kinds of writing and taping. I often speculate as to why. Is it because many teachers despise young people's culture? Is it because they don't think it's 'important'? Is it because education is supposed to be about giving something to children, not about taking something from them? Is it because many teachers organise classrooms in such a way that interviews and taping and group writing and performing and discussing don't seem possible? Is it because all this stuff seems threatening and could cause children to start throwing things and jumping out of windows?

From the young person's point of view the situation might seem like this:

> I am sitting here in this classroom and you don't seem to be interested in what I do, where I do it, who I meet, my beliefs, my way of talking. You then ask me to write about 'The week-end' or 'A bad day'. I can't do it. You will not be an interested audience.

On the other hand, when the cultural identity of the young person is received with interest, 'many flowers bloom'. In my experience, the 'flowers' have been of many kinds: a study of black history, for instance, a set of poems by a young girl about her relationship with her mother, a book of 'my dad's stories' and so on. In each case, the starting-out point was an interchange about 'culture'.

So what am I saying? There has been a lot of interest taken in the bad 'isms' of education — racism, sexism, classism. But central to the problem, it seems to me, is an adult versus childism. We don't actually like children's or young people's culture. To which I would say, how the hell are we supposed to set about any of the other three 'isms' if there isn't the respect for the child in the first place, believed in and shown by the encouragement of writing and taping of the kind I have illustrated?

The result of our ignoring their culture, combined with the constant injection of 'our stuff', is that we choose to influence young people with adult-chosen culture. For many schools this means the culture of the dominant white male media. For some schools, it may mean non-dominant forms are represented. That's fine as far as it goes. But any young person will find it difficult to engage with even these non-dominant forms if their own culture (also non-dominant!) is not given space. Young people have to have the chance to confront new ideas using the tools that they produce.

APPENDIX II
Children's Poems Plus Notes

My Room Cleaning
Mum told me to clean my room up.
But I didn't.
Instead I danced to John Farnham
On my radio cassette.
I didn't know Mum was trying to sleep
And my radio was on Full Bore!!!! [Ball]
Boy!!!
WAS SHE MAD!!!

Rebecca

This came out of a one-off workshop. I performed a set of poems about sharing my bedroom with my brother; getting into a clothes fight with him; my dad coming in and telling us off; my brother imitating my dad; us getting into trouble again when we were doing the washing up and spraying water at each other; my dad coming in and telling us off; my brother imitating my dad behind his back.

I then showed the children about how to lay words out on the page in a way that helps the person read it in the way you want them to. I showed them Buffalo Bill's (see page 37) and 'Slow Children Crossing' (see page 37). Then I asked the children to recall what kinds of things I had just been performing. Out of this arose a loose set of cues or titles, like: 'Getting into trouble', 'My room', etc.

I then said, 'When you write about something that's happened to you don't forget to write down the things that people say, and the things that you think.'

Notes on the poem: Rebecca has ignored my plea to write down what people say and what you think and chosen to put it into voice monologue. I like it because it feels real to her experience, she names names — it's not just 'a record' but 'John Farnham', she uses her dialect 'full ball' and her spoken voice; 'WAS SHE MAD', and she has devised her own punctuation '!!!!'

---

*My Brother the Dobber**
My brother is a dobber.
I go and buy a packet of Twisties and he says:
'If you don't give me some Twisties, I'll dob.'
But when he buys something, I say:
'If you don't give me —'
Then he interrupts and says:
'I don't care.'
Why does it work for him, but not for me?'

Simone Beitmans

* Dobbing = 'telling on someone', 'grassing', 'squeling', 'singing,.

This arose out of a newspaper article that a teacher read. I had been interviewed by a local newspaper in Perth, Australia and I had very briefly outlined what I have described in the notes to the previous poem. She then went to her class and put it in her own words and asked them to write. This is what came out.

Notes on the poem: It deals with real dilemmas and problems of day to day life of children in their relationships with each other and their parents. 'Dobbing' is a crucial issue for children in relation to authority. Simone is able to catch the feeling of the matter by using both what people say and her own thought on the matter.

Neil Wheatley said:
Some people call me 'Weetabix'.
Paulette said:

My nickname is 'Record Player'
because my last name is Rickard.
Paul Thorne's dad says to him:
'Tommy Gun, can you get
a cup of tea,
because he always plays army.
Christopher Barrow calls his mum,
'Fag Ash Lil'
because she flicks ash everywhere.
Jason Baker's mum's friends call her 'Taxi'
because her initials are 'C.A.B.'
And there's
'Honk Honk' because her name's Hornet;
the Grandad called 'Wasp'
because he found a wasp's nest,
'Sloon' because when he was small
that's how he said 'Spoon',
'Forget-it' because she forgets things,
'Green Cheese' because he always wants
what other people ask for
and Titch No. 3 because
she's the third smallest in class.
My nickname is Branston
because
my second name is Nicholls
so they call me Pickles
because it rhymes with Nicholls
and Branston Pickles.

We all have nicknames
And so have I.
My mother calls me Flash Gordon
because I am so slow.
My father says I have two speeds:
dead slow and stop.
All my friends call me
Mulhollybush
because I have so much hair.

My sister calls me D.D.
because when she first came into the world
she said affectionately, D.D.
A teacher in my school calls me
Staffan Rabonski.
I do not know why.
We all have nicknames.
And so do I.

                              Stephen Mulholland

In a national Sunday newspaper, I had a monthly column
for children. On this occasion, I told the children about
nicknames that my friends and relations had given me,
and put in my poem 'Juster and Waiter' from 'You Can't
Catch Me'. I then asked the readers to send in their nicknames and how they got them. I then made a compilation,
just as one could do in a class, out of them.

   Nicknames are about identity. In the context of a class it
can be opened out into the issue of name calling and the
jostling for power that all that implies: as in the following
poem:

My brother says bad words to me
'Khabish'
I say
'Naughty boy'
'I'm going to tell my Mum'
so my Mum hits him
and my Mum calls him
'Monkey'
My sister calls me
'Cat'
'a black monkey'
and
'a rat'
I never say anything to anyone.

                                        by Asma

Tracy Argent, the language post holder at the school wrote this: 'Working with Selima, the Bengali mother tongue teacher, Bridget, the class teacher and two children who speak Bengali as a first language, Mike "discovered" that he too could scribe in Bengali using English script. This opens up all sorts of possibilities for the mono-lingual teacher (able at some point to work with a bi-lingual teacher) as, for example, the child who does not feel sufficiently confident to relate an experience in English, can do so in her/his first language and see it "happening on paper".'

I've since worked with Greek speaking children in Canada who wrote the narrative of the poem in English and all the home dialogue in Greek.

When I was only about 10
I always wanted to play football
with my big brother
and all his big friends.
So he said,
'If you come, and you get hurt,
and come and complain to me
you'll never come with me again.'
So the next day I got all my football gear ready
and I went out with my brother
thinking that I looked so good —
big.
But when we got there
the size of the other team was frightening —
big.
and I began to get a bit worried.
I felt so big when I was mouthing
around but when it came to it
I felt so small.

Thomas Ioannou, (13)

I worked with a group of boys in a London Secondary school on the idea of bullies and being made to feel small. Or — a bit nearer to the bone — pretending to be big when inside you felt quite small. This is a poem that came out of that talk.

I was sitting watching the tele,
I was interested in the film —
It was the Magnificent Five —
When my Mum said:
'Switch the door off and shut the light.'
My brother Simon has a bullet
Which he wears on a thong around his neck.
He started wearing this at night, in bed,
As well as during the day time.
Mum and Dad were both worried about this.
Mum was going on and on about it and she said:
'If you wake up dead in the morning...!'

When my brother was six,
He'd been watching an operation on TV
About a lady who was having her kidneys removed.
Later he was trying to tell me about it and said:
'Jamie, you know that lady who
Had her mushrooms removed...'

Our school was putting on a play called Tom Sawyer.
The boy who was playing Huckleberry Finn said:
'I'll have to wash my hair and brush my face.'

One day our mam was in a rush
To make the beds, make the dinner
And get out.
She said:
'Go upstairs
And wash the door
And shut your face.'

Matthew Drury said,
After it had been snowing,
'I've just been snowing throwballs.'

I was ironing my clothes and mum said:
'Put that iron back in the fridge!'

My teacher said:
'Get the board and
Put the date on the chalk.'

Collecting 'fluffs' (as verbal mistakes are known-in the
Theatre business) is great fun and quite revealing. One
teacher I know (hallo Rod!) made a non-stop wall poster
out of them with mad illustrations to match. This one
comes from readers of my column in the Sunday paper.

A New Area
I came here from not so far away
New faces to stare at.
Everybody laughing at my Lancashire accent.
A different way of living.
No hills here, no mills, no chimneys.
A house in the countryside.
I soon made friends and knew who to trust.
Everybody crowding round me looking
at my writing, weighing me up.
Everybody saying that I'm a good footballer.
Glad to have me in the team.

Matthew Butler (11)

Moving In
Moving out
Of an old crowd
trying
to move
Into a new crowd
But no one

112

wants to know
you
At all.

But when
you make them
feel stupid
And make them
look small
Everybody
wants to be your friend
Everybody
wants to be your friend
Everyone around
you
You seem to know.

Marisa Horsford (12)

These two poems were written in response to my poem 'Newcomers'. 'My father came to England...' etc. in 'Quick let's Get out of Here.'

I don't know how Marisa Horsford arrived at a form that puts it in the present tense and with the repetitions that represent how she's thinking. She was a published poet at eleven. Of course, it is a form that one can show other children, but ideally it should grow from the situation.

The Pig Sty By Jon Rundle

"OH MY GOD!"
JOOON! GET UP HERE"
The voice echos
first down the stairs,
and then it rumbles to my ears.
"Here we go again"
I start to creep up the stairs
But

113

Its no good
Shes there,
The stare is like a laser beam,
Cutting through me
"Jo...."

"I know - the room, - I'm coming"
"I want that room spic and span In 1 HOUR!"
I start

Aha!,
A backdating Beano,
"Jon You have 45 mins"

I start again,
I find some Blu-Tak,
"Where are those two posters?"

I spend another 10 mins finding them,
"Jon, 30 minutes
"Yer"

I start again,
I stop again,
Aha, Plasticine

114

Flick,
I find a target
A teddy,
Yeh, On the head.
"Jon the time is nearly up"
I scamper around

picking up things
stuffing them in drawers, anywhere
I hear her coming upstairs
I get on my bed and lay there,
She opens the door
"Very good, dinners ready"

by Jon Rundle

Tidying up is a great 'theme' to raise with children as it is
such a battleground in family life. Who is going to do it,
who is going to try and get out of doing it, what tricks do
people get up to to avoid doing it and so on. This one came
out of a one-off school visit workshop. I think it captures
the two people: mum and himself each going along their
separate tracks. The pay-off at the end is very well managed.

My best friend's leaving.
It's not fair.
He's a fourth year.
I'm a third year.
My best friend's Steven.
He's a really groovy mate.
Will I still be able to be friends with him?
I'll just have to accept that he's leaving
It's badly out of order.
Well, at least I'll have other friends
staying.

by Joseph Bentley

A discussion arose with children leaving primary school, to go to secondary school at the age of eleven. This poem is the thinking-out-loud type where the language represents spoken reasoning rather than 'stream of consciousness'. A kind of internal dialogue. Note that it arises out of the real situation that Joseph is going through — that's why it sounds good.

The Wall
In our school
There's a long brick wall
'That has to come down'
Says that fat cruel man
'We're making two-bedroom flats.'
'Oh no' we say
'You can't do that
Just leave us alone
And go away'
'That must come down'
Says the fat cruel man
'We're making two-bedroom flats'
We sigh and say
'We can't do nothing about it'

by Mehtap Abdullah

The class teacher, Penny Bentley, had been dealing with this wall for some time. This poem and many others didn't simply arise out of 'Let's go and look at the wall'. A whole debate about the wall, the rights and wrongs of it being demolished and neighbourhood politics came into the discussion.

When I was 7
I went to heaven
when I was 8
I got a date
When I was 9
I got a fine
When I was 10
I swallowed a pen
Well that's what I am that what
I'll be with a Tony To — To-ny

Tony was into rapping. I seem to have mislaid 1-6! He was a lad who had problems about ever wanting to write anything, but rapping and rhyming appealed to him. We grabbed it while the enthusiasm was high.

My Dad
When my dad is on nights
he wakes up with
a grumble
he says
where's my tea?
where's the paper?
I don't say
one
little
word.
I get grumbled at
all daylong,
till he goes to work.

And the next day's
the same

by Helen Adams

My Mom
When my mom's in the kitchen
frying sausages
I come in and peep over
the frying pan
and the fat spits
everywhere.
It burns my nose
and I cry.
my mom rubs it better
and says
dear dear
you won't die.

by Kathy Eims

My sister
My sister's
a nuisance
She screams
Where's my tea
When she comes home from work

She cries
After sloppy films

My sister's
a nuisance
On Saturday
I had some NEW perfume
She cried to my mum
She's too young
to have perfume.

In bed is the worst part
She shouts
Oh I've forgotten
to go to
the toilet
She runs downstairs

my sister's
a nuisance

by Debra Mills

Jan, then a classroom teacher in Birmingham, got hold of
'Mind Your Own Business', read them the poems and got
the class talking about brothers and sisters and mums and
dads and what really goes on.

———————————

I was naughty once
One time when we were going to have dinner
Mum said will you lay the table please
and I said NO
mum said
If
you
don't
LAY
the table

you will not have dinner
then dad came in
and said what is going on
then I said I don't know Dad.

by Nicola Tew

The day I was ~~annoying~~ annoying my mum

one day my mum says
do you want your friends to come round
to play
and I say yes please
So then my mum rings them up
but then she stopped
because she could here a noise
so she said
if you dont stop that before, I
conut To ten
I will not call your friends round
1 2 3 4 5 6 7 8 9 10
there was silence
then the noise started agian   then she
Said
I told you to stop that
then I say
you have counted to ten
thats what we are started agian

Mark
McDermott

120

When I was naughty.

One day
I got out of bed in a bad mood.
because my brother woke me up.
"Why did you have to do that"!
I said it so loud
that I woke my mother and father up.
"Calm down, Calm down."
This is where the argument started.
"But mum, he started it." I said
"He's younger than you he's only five."
At "I hate you"
Mum was so cross with me now
that she said
"You better watch your manners, young lady."
I think that my mum likes my brother best.

by
Susana Castellot

Naughtiness and arguments always raise the crunchy issues in families so long as we get down to the real nitty-gritty of what actually takes place. These were written after one-off workshops of the kind I've already described.

I am ill
I feel sick
in Bed
I see a bird
flying around outside the window
I hear my brothers playing
Mu-u-u-m
I want some thing to eat
I'm thinking
I wish I was playing
with my brothers

by Nicola

ill
sick
in bed
a bird
flying around outside the window
my brother playing
m-u u m
i want something to eat thinking
i wish i was playing
with my brothers

by Nicola

Shopping with my mum
shopping
got lost
scared
frightened
people talking
lots of legs walking
around
Me
mu — um mu — um
found you
ho good

by Nicola

people talking
people eating
people fiting
people tripping
people crying
peoples' legs
people running
people playing
people walking dogs
people bumping into eachothe

by Thomas

This sequence of poems is quite revealing. They came out
of several sessions with the same group of children —
seven year olds. The first 'I am ill', by Nicola arose out of
the present tense idea I describe on p.67. The second poem
comes out of talking through with her the idea of simply
writing the answers to the questions 'what can you see'
and not having to write 'I can see ...' etc each time. The
group discussed it and tried both ways of writing and
choosing which they liked best and why. Then we did getting lost, and Nicola chose to write it in a stream of consciousness style straightaway. Then Thomas takes off on
his own, inventing his own form, putting little cartoons at
the end of each line of the poem to illustrate what he's
describing.

when we used to stay in Number 5
and once I went to Number 6
when I went near the lift
I saw a man then.
The man hold my hand.
Then I said come in
in Bengali
he was English
he did not understand me
I said come in
Because I thought he was a good
man
but he wasn't a good man
he wanted to take me away.
Then I ran home
then I said to my mum The Thing
Then she said
Don't go any more

by Beauty

The first version of this went something like this:

'When we used to stay in Number 5 I saw a man and I said
come in.'

It was written as part of us talking about things we're
afraid of and times we've been afraid.

I told Beauty that I didn't understand what she had
written, so I 'interviewed' her and wrote down exactly
what she said in reply to my questions.

———————————

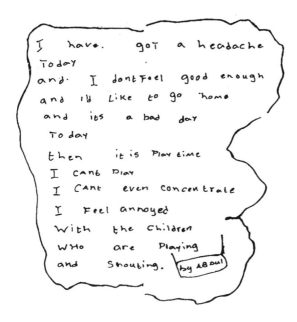

I have got a headache
Today
and I dont Feel good enough
and id Like to go home
and its a bad day
To day

then it is Play time
I cant Play
I cant even concentrate
I Feel annoyed
With the Children
Who are Playing
and Shouting. by ABoul

Abdul (7) is feeling his way towards a form with the repetition of 'today', the rhyme that happens naturally and the rhythm of the last four words. We don't have to impose form on children all the time. They start inventing their own.

One day
when I was little
I was playing in the sand
I saw an ugly man
he said:
do you want an apple?
I said: No
and I ran away
I went home
I said to my mum
about everything that happened.

125

My mum said:
He is a Kuskur
He chops people's heads off
Then I was scared
then I didn't go again.

by Akaddus

If we get children to write down what people really say, we start getting into their oral culture and the oral culture of the people around them. Out of the blue, Akaddus revealed this folk character 'Kuskur'. The other children soon chipped in with their Kuskur stories that we wrote down.

———————————

One night
after going to a fancy-dress party
dressed as a carrot
I saw a giant rabbit.
It thought I was his dinner.
While I was running away from it,
I fell.
I could not get up.
My leg bled
The giant rabbit hopped nearer to me.
It opened his mouth
and wanted to eat me up.
When his teeth touched my head
I woke up
and found myself on the floor.
I think that must have happened
when I fell.

by Ho Foong Ling
That was a nightmare told for real.

———————————

I can hear the grandfather clock strike twelve
The dog starts to howl
I see and hear thunder and lightning
After dark, after dark
The wind blows — I think it's a ghost
I see the door of my closet moving
I hear someone screaming
After dark, after dark
The wind blows — I think it's a ghost
I see the door of my closet moving
I hear someone screaming
After dark, after dark
The eyes on a portrait stare at me
Something is moving, something is peeping, through the
window
A big black spider is hanging over my bed
After dark, after dark
Watching horror movies frightens me
Someone walks past my bedroom door as I try to sleep
I see the shadow of banana leaves hanging around
After dark, after dark
I see the tree moving in the backyard
The earthquake makes me feel so frightened
Cockroaches are walking on my body
After dark, after dark
There's a carpet that is rolled like a mummy in my bed-
room
And my bed makes a strange noise that makes me scared
to go the toilet
Hidden eyes are watching me from everywhere
After dark, after dark

This is a class poem, each student writing his or her own
single line. The students were second language speakers,
Japanese, Swedish, Italian and others in an international
school in Singapore.

Penny:	Goodnight
Us:	Goodnight Miss.
Penny:	I'll put Joseph's slipper at the door to keep it open.
Joseph:	Why?
Penny:	To let the light in.
	(Then Penny went out)
	Christopher coughed.
Steven:	Shut up Christopher.
Christopher:	What's the time Steven?
Steven:	I don't know. I can't see.
Christopher:	Brian, are you asleep?
Brian:	I'm not now, am I?

by Brian Bellerby

I was working with some children who had just come back from their school journey. We soon got into talking about who got up to what in the dormitories. So I suggested we write dialogues that take place in the dormitory. Trips and outings ARE often a stimulus for writing, but I like to find the parts of the trip or outing where relationships are being worked through.

Brussels and Peas
Here's me
I'm sitting at home.
Then in comes DINNER.

Oh no.
Peas and those horrible Brussels.

Those green little things.

Those big mushy things,
one thing I hate most is those
Brussels and peas.

I'm not eating them.
Yes you are
I'm not.
Yes you are or you're not to go out.

Here goes.
1 pea on the fork
Look at it.
Smell it.
Eat it.
YUK!

Here goes brussels.

1 on the fork
Look at it.
Smell it.
Eat it.
YUK!

Rumble rumble rumble.
Down my mouth they go.

I'm not eating them,
they're dreadful, thought me.

Here goes a second one.

Round green and horrible.
Down my tunnel it goes.
YUK YUK YUK

I did not eat my peas all up
I did not eat my Brussels.
But I never went out.
Green nasty big things
Green nasty little things.

Never
will I touch a pea
or a brussel again.
YUK! YUK! YUK!

By Kelly Daniels

Food is terribly important. Kelly was someone who took everything at great speed, and was a bit slapdash about writing so by getting her to put the episode into the present tense she had to slow down and take one pea at a time!

Don't leave the liver in the river
Don't worry about the curry
Don't put a loo in your shoe
Don't be silly with chilli
Don't give the mice your rice
Don't eat Biryani when its sunny
Don't make Karl eat Dahl*
Don't put a bee on my knee

by Shazina Begum

My 'Don't' poem in 'Don't put the Mustard in the Custard' was used as a cue here to have a bit of rhyming fun. It's nice to see her being free with her own culture.

Looking Forward to Eid
Absolutely buried in money
sweets, cakes.
Aunties hugging you 'UGH'
New clothes
Relatives visiting you
and your getting squashed
Oh you've grown up haven't you
going everywhere
well nearly everywhere

* I think she means 'dal' not Roald but who cares?!

Presents
Optimus prime giant figure
every mask toy
toy cars
thundercats toys
toy fire engine
and a great big football.
Going to the Mosque
if you forget
your prayers
then you've had it
and your parents say
the more you get hit
the more you learn.

by Malik

Looking forward to something is a feeling that children experience frequently. I have found that one way to get to it is through the present tense method: Yoo are now looking forward to that special thing... how do you feel? What are you thinking? What's going to happen? Malik's poem is good because it is so specific to the actual objects and actual things that people will say. The fact that he gets away from conventional sentences helps it feel more immediate and breathless.

———————

Crackers and Cheese
When we were having crackers for tea
my sister sometimes throws crumbs under the table
under my seat
so I have to sweep them up
I feel angry
So I go upstairs
and get my rubber spider out of my bedroom
and put it in my sister's bed.
When dad reads her her night story
she gets right down in her bed.
She looks

then she jumps out of her skin.
Hee hee haw haw.

by Jonathan Gibbons

Revenge is a good theme. Or 'Getting your own back' as children know it. I once put a twig in my brother's bed. I told Jonathan about it *after* he had written his poem not before. Poems open conversations.

———————————

High Woman
She knows she's in a white man's land
She holds her head up high
Some think quite low of her
But she makes them think high

She walks with dignity
peace and grace
Surely she belongs
in the human race.

She nuh president
but she has a resident
to occupy her time.
Sweet woman, sweet woman
High woman of mine.

by Judith Ellis

Judith was a storyteller who told a range of Jamaican stories that she had mostly learnt from her mother. At one point I asked her to take a tape recorder home and tape her mother telling stories. This she did and her mother told them in 'patois', the Jamaican dialect. We transcribed Judith's telling of the stories and put them in the school library. She started writing poems. This one is about her mother which she wrote when she was about fourteen. It was published along with ten others in 'Black Ink', 258 Coldharbour Lane, London SW9, UK. Last time I heard of her she was reading this poem on a TV programme.

———————————

God of Tower Blocks
I am Spirit of Tower Blocks
My name is Bang
I make tower blocks collapse
When I like
And people who live in the tower blocks
Haven't got any lifts that work
Because I break them
And the children haven't got
A playground
To play in
because I don't let them
So they have a lot of noise.

by Ikenna

I am the God of Sport
My name is the Best of the Rest

When teams are bad I make
Them lose and the good team wins

I help Daly Thompson at the Pole Vault.
He runs about 25 metres
Then he bends the pole on the floor
When the pole is ready he throws
Himself over the bar

I helped when John Barnes crossed
The ball and Gary Lineker chested
It down to his foot and scored

I helped Ian Botham when
He kept on getting sixes and fours
He hits the ball off the pitch
Without it touching the floor
He enjoys himself
I am THE BEST OF THE REST

by Carlton

I am Novess
I am the God of November
I make all the leaves
Fall off the trees
I make the weather turn cold
I make the day shorter
And the night longer
I make all the people
Wear woolly clothes
And big coats
I make lots of people buy fireworks
And go to the park
And
　　let
　　　them
　　　　go!!!

by Lee

I am Trick
I can do nasty trick and good tricks and this is how it
goes
I can make people go away
I can turn people into pigs
And
I can turn water into blood
I can make people sit on snakes
I can make children be rude to their parents
I go around people's houses and knock things over.

by Susan

My Name is Happiness
I make people laugh
When people are sad I cheer them up
I tickle people without them knowing
And make them laugh
I make funny jokes
Like:
Knock Knock

134

Who's there?
Des
Des who?
Des no bell, that's why I'm knocking
HA
  HA
    HA
      HA
 I pull funny faces and make people laugh
I make funny noises and make
them laugh.

by Kim

This group of poems comes from the idea of asking children to pretend to be more powerful than they are. I'm asking them to pretend to be in control, either as a spirit, a goddess, a god or whatever. Rather than ask them to do strange and fantastic things, I try to get them to focus on the things that actually happen around them. I should add, it's not meant to be a serious explanation of how these phenomena really do happen but a much more playful idea than that!

My Nightmare
It is night. I am walking home. I can hear someone behind me. It is starting to run. I start to run faster and faster. I run round the corner. I shout. No one can hear me. I knock on all the doors. Men come. I stop knocking on the door. I run from a bus but I miss it. I run in a church. The thing shouted. I was shaking. I had to look at him. I looked, It was horrible. It had 4 arms, 1 eye, 3 legs. I got a candelabra. He came to me. I hit him on the head and then I woke up.

by Peter Gardiner

This is work on *real* nightmares: 'Please don't *make up* a nightmare, today'(!) I've left it in the format he wrote it, but it obviously cries out for free verse presentation.

The Squashed Hedgehog
I am a hedgehog
it's dark
very dark
I am going across a road
the owl hoots
I look up
there's a noise behind me
I look round
There's bright lights shining in my eye
I am motionless.
The car's coming nearer
the lights
the bright lights
the wheel's on my foot
I feel terrible pain
the pain
the pain's creeping up my body
the pain's terrible
I am dying
In a fraction of a second I will be dead.

by Gary Young

The Tiger
Here I am in a cage
small and cramped.
Once I was free out in the wild
But now I am in the London Zoo.
I wish I was out in the wild with all my mates.
I was once but then the white man came and caught me
and put me in a cage.
I used to run, leap and hunt.
But now I only get one plate of meat a day.
Here I am looked at and sometimes someone throws

things at me.
I used to play out in the wild and enjoy myself,
but here I am stuck up in this small, untidy, cramped
cage.

by Barry Dunne

I once wrote a poem called 'I am a wasp', in 'Wouldn't You Like to Know?' which describes a wasp caught in a wasp trap. Here I've given the children a chance to explore the position of victim. As I remember it, it partly arose out of a situation in a boys' school where there was a lot of bullying going on and I thought that a bit of identification with the victim might help.

The Day I Got My Own Back
It was my birthday and I got a watch. It was a good watch and I had had it for only one week when my brother threw it at me. I went to catch it but I missed and it hit a cupboard door and fell on the floor. When I went to pick it up, I saw that it had stopped. I picked it up and I started to wind it up but it just wouldn't go so I said to my brother, 'Not to tell my mum,' and he said, 'OK.' — and went off and told my dad instead. I waited a minute or two and then my dad came in and told me off so I had to get my own back — so the next morning I got up very very early, got my pillow and hit my brother over the head with it and woke him and I said, 'Time for school,' and then I got back into bed.

Anyway, my brother got up, got dressed for school and then I shouted, 'IT'S SATURDAY, YOU TWIT!'

by Barry

Here the issue of 'Revenge' is dealt with by an eleven year old. I told them the story of 'The Twig in the Bed' in 'Quick let's Get Out of Here'.

Irritating Sayings

Go and take the dog out
go and get the newspapers
go and clean your room out
go to your room
make sure you eat your school dinner
eat with your mouth shut
no more lip
you just cheese me off sometimes
don't come funny
sit down and shut up
don't keep on or else
clean your teeth
go and do your homework
make sure you eat your school dinner
don't be cheeky
money doesn't grow on trees
when I was your age we had no money
it's all your fault
make sure you're in by nine
you'll never get up in the morning
don't talk with your mouth full
 N — O — spells no
want, want, want, — that's all you ever say
I'm not putting the snooker table away
hurry up and get out of the bath
don't forget to pull the plug
shut up — stop talking about war
you're late where you been?
bang bang pop pop — that's all you say
war, war, war — SHUT UP
it's time for work not playing
go and do your homework
stop playing with Kerry and go to the shop for me
look at me when I'm talking to you
what's the time? It's well past your bedtime
don't talk with your mouth full
it's all your fault

don't give me any lip
you make me sick
go and take a running jump
sh! I'm listening to the news
time for bed — have you forgotten about school
tomorrow?
don't give me none of your cheek
money doesn't grow on trees
when I was your age I never got helped as much as
you
stop beating up your sister
get out of your room or get to bed
stop being silly
stop backchatting
go and take the dog out
I'll clump you
don't get too near the telly
you don't know your right from left
don't cut things on the table
your dinner's getting cold
where's my shoes gone
go to the shop for me
you're going deaf
I want to watch football.
I want to watch the film
mum! tell him he keeps picking on me
you won't get up in the morning for school
now look what you've done
don't answer me back
shush! I'm watching the television
don't go away — your dinner will be ready soon
mum can I stay out for ten minutes more?
do your homework
go to bed
go and wash
go to the shop
go away for the hundredth time
now what are you doing?

you're not even watching the football
it's all your fault
if you don't hurry up you'll be late for school
don't talk to me like that
cheeky monkey
go and make a cup of tea for me
don't stay up too late — school tomorrow
Oi — homework
you make up
when I was your age I was making tea for your
Uncle David
get out of the kitchen
don't keep talking about cats and cars, Paul
when I was your age we never had that much money
hold your knife and fork right
don't talk with your mouth full
make your bed
stop watching television
it's all your fault
my mum said eat your dinner in the kitchen
Gordon and Karl always make trouble
hey Pat, what's the time? around bed-time isn't it?
not ain't isn't
not yeah — yes
put the milk bottles out
don't be cheeky to your older brother
go and buy the newspaper
turn the TV off or go to bed. Which one?
Listen to me when I'm talking
make me coffee
go to bed now and don't talk
put all your toys away
I don't want any of your cheek
make your tea
do this, do that
sit down and shut up
I was good when I was little
did anybody ask your opinion

Ricky — pay attention
go and buy the newspaper
don't let me see you do that again
you shouldn't need telling at your age
go and sit down and stop moaning
it's too late
go and play with the traffic
go and do your homework
you're lucky to get any
stop moving the chair
no buts
move out of the way
hop to it
N-O-, spells 'no'
move yourself
no more lip from you
stop swinging on the chair
wash your hands
do the washing up
it's nothing to do with you
mind your own business
respect your elders
on your bike
nag, nag, nag
get up for school
B — E — D, spells 'bed'
because I say so
have you made your bed?
shut up or else
that is stupid
when I was your age
I got half as much as you did
what did I tell you?

This is a class compilation piece on the kinds of things parents say to you. Compilation pieces are great for showing what is actually possible and 'legal' to put down on a page. Lists of phrases, words, expletives, and the like can then be acted out or presented in a dramatic form in some way, tape-slide or whatever. It's very useful for first writers, or reluctant writers.

———————————

The Outing
We went on an outing
to London Zoo.

We was having
a great time.

My mate Dominic
he bought a stick of rock

We went to the gorillas —
they like sweets.

My mate Dominic
he got the rock

He was messing about
with the gorillas.

My teacher said,
'NO ONE
IS ALLOWED TO MESS ABOUT WITH THE
GORILLAS.
DON'T GIVE THEM SWEETS.'

My friend was messing about
with the rock and the gorilla

and then the gorilla
caught the rock.
and he was pulling it

and the gorilla
ate it all up —
and he wasn't allowed to.

And my teacher, Miss Grills said, to my mate,
'When you get back to school,
YOU'VE HAD IT'

Nicky Papapetrou

What actually takes place on school outings may not be the
scientific or empirical study that was intended. Or the
empirical work takes place, but what really *fascinates* is an
event or moment like this one.

My Daydream
My daydream is about when I had a truck. I was
working with my friend Eddie. And at the back of
the truck was a go-kart with an engine in it. That
go-kart was a special go-kart. It was like James
Bond's car. And I parked my car at the bottom of the
sea and then my mum woke me up!

by Joseph Colucci

Real daydreams are worth trying to get hold of. Here I
haven't made the most of the daydream in that if I had got
Joseph to put it into the present tense, it might have felt
more immediate and he would have got nearer to the spirit
of it. I sometimes describe this process to children as wind-
ing back the video and running it again. No matter how
many times you wind it back, the action is always happening for the first time: in the present, now.

Grendel
Grendel had a horn on his nose with big, ugly teeth
and sharp claws and hot looking eyes. He also had a
great strong tail with spikes along his tail and all up
his back. Big ugly nostrils and horrible black
blotches over his back. The colour of his skin is
green with slimy green moss and seaweed all over
him.

by Karen Jeffs

A class of fourteen year old girls were doing Anglo-Saxon history, so I offered to tell them the story of Beowulf. What I then suggested was that they simply imagine what Grendel looks like. The epic-poem only gives glimpses of him 'grim and greedy', but the dramatic situations are very graphic. To imagine Grendel, I gave the girls a chance to put some of their fears into a concrete literary situation.

I think Karen's piece could do with some more work, laying it out on the page in free verse form and asking her some more questions about Grendel. Drama work would have helped a lot here.

Hospital
Me no wan you, bout man
soon as me tun me back
you go pick up man pan you self
and now you pregnant.
When you come out
me no want you back a yard again.
Now you come tell me you pregnant
and you don't even know
who de fader is.
A wha' wrong with children nowadays
dem tink dem no everytink
but dem don't.
So you and de baby
bettar go fine house
and live.

by Veronica

I was seeing a class of sixteen year old girls who were remedial writers and readers. I told them a story about how when I was in hospital seeing my wife and new born baby boy I had seen a scene where a young black girl in the next door bed had been waiting for her mum to come and see her and her new born baby. A few minutes later, in came mum and suddenly all hell broke loose, there was shouting and screaming and clearly mum was not pleased.

I told the girls that I couldn't really understand what was being said. 'What do you think mum was saying?', I asked.

'There was banging at the front door.
Bricks came through the window
The mother gathered her children.
She picked up the phone
but they had cut the wire.
'Hooligans', she cried.
She cried for help.
The neighbours came out.
One neighbour had a shot gun and fired it at their feet.
When the police came, they took no interest and said,
"We can't help you."'

There had been some racist abuse and attacks at the school, so I brought in a book by Amrit Wilson in which she prints the oral testimony of Bangladeshi women in the east end of London describing attacks on them ('Finding a Voice' Virago). I then suggested that they write things from the point of view of those women. This method had been criticised for being victim orientated rather than looking at ways of overcoming racism, and getting children to work on that. I agree with that and think that work like this piece by a boy could be stage one of this process, stage two being 'what shall we do?'

The Day It Happened
It happened. I never thought it would have
  I was talking to a friend,
    There was going to be a fight with these boys.
      The fight started

The white boys were getting beaten up.
  A police car. Oh NO everyone scatter
    The police jump out grabbing a black boy
      Throwing him to the ground.

Needing help they radio for more police men.
  In a few seconds they arrive
    They didn't have to do that.
      The teachers could have sorted it out
        There and then

But NO they got arrested!
  I never thought they would
    I felt so helpless
      I didn't know what to do.

I was scared, shocked and concerned for the boys.
  I cried that day, I cried.
    I never thought it would have happened.
      Not to US!

by Susan Hamilton

Here's the school event. (See page 49) A gang of white boys came over to the predominantly black school I was working at and attacked a group of black boys outside school. What took place went through the school like lightning and simply could not be ignored, especially in times when children were being asked to think about writing.

Oh Mother!
'If you're going out, brush your teeth
and don't leave toothpaste all over the sink
Oh — and change your socks — there are some in the boiler room.
If you want some money — it's on the table
Only take two pounds
And put it in the pocket with a zip,
Have a good time, love
But no hanky panky and...
  'Oh Mother!'

by Adam

We were talking serious teenage love and going out, but Adam chose to focus on what mum says.

Dancing Machine
I'm a dancing machine
It only takes one thing to turn me on
And that's music
I'm a machine who wants to do one thing
And that's dance
I could achieve fame by doing what I do
And that's dance
Come on let's dance
Put all your sorrows aside and let's dance
Put all your troubles aside and let's dance
Come on let's dance. Turn on the music and let's dance.

by Doreen

I think it's important that children get a chance to write
their own pop songs and ideally get a chance to hear them
performed.

Seeing Grandad Dead
We are all in the room
His hands over his will
Says goodbye
As he falls back on the bed dead.
A big scream takes over
My dad calms us
And says
One day we all have to die.

The day ends with everyone crying
The next day he is buried.

In a few days it is forgotten in the outside
But not in the inside
Everyone's forgotten about that terrible day
And we are back to normal.

Ladi Mohammed

Seeing Death
I was home for dinner
my uncle was at home
crying
My grandmother and my auntie
just came from the hospital
They came in crying
and said to me
'Your cousin has died today
in the hospital.'
The following Wednesday
they brought the body home
Everyone crying
when he came in the house
my heart started to beat
Harder and harder
I felt very weak
I felt like dying as well
and the baby was so cold and bright
They were about to take it away
when the mother said,
'Don't take my child away from me!'

by Sanjay Patel

I saw a dead man on Euston station and came in and told
the children about it. Several children had experiences
that overlapped with it.

Farewell India
My mum says
 I miss my friends
  And long long talks
   And nice sunny days
    The sky so far away
     From the Indian earth.

My mum says
 I miss our farm
  our big big farm
   where we grew wheat
    sugar cane, corn, and rice
     and palm trees reached up tall

My mum says
 India I miss you
 And your warm heart

by Pravir Gami

My Mum Says
My mum says
  We're moving because it is too noisy
  And she says she would like to move
  to the country

My mum says
  that it's easy to walk
  and easy to the town centre

My mum says
  that it's a quiet place
  and it's easy to get to school

by Terry Mowland

My Memories
Bangladesh
I remember going to my village home
I remember it being hot
I remember the soles of my shoes
burning up on the hot road
I remember jumping about because
of my hot foot
I remember my little brother
running up to my grandparents
on his little feet like an ant

I remember my little brother
jumping on my grandfather's lap
and my grandfather nearly falling
off the chair
I remember having a nice meal
I remember my brother eating
the leg of a chicken like a lion
eating a deer
I remember the homemade ovens
I remember... I remember...
I remember... I remember BANGLADESH

by Tanweer Khaled

My Second Home!
Smells of you draw me to you
   The smell of fish
Vegetables and Kebab
The smell of sea
The smell of Cyprus that I want
to smell
That's not all I want to do
I want to see the sea that's blue
The sky too
I want to see the green leaves
from the tree

Cyprus is my second home
we eat
 vegetables, meat
  white beans
 kebab, taramasalata
 meatballs, kollogasin
and all kinds of cheeses and fish
 we get all these things from
the market, but we get a fish market
on its own

The smell of Cyprus draws me
to it.
   The smell of grass, trees and leaves
The colours are so bright, the sky is a
different blue from England
   If only I was there right now
to see and smell all these things
which I can't smell in England.

by Joanna Eracleous

Cows
The cow that wanders has nothing to eat
The cow that has a home has everything
The cow that's in a farm gets bored
The cow that wanders is homeless
The cow is happy and gentle at home
The cow that is sold always comes
   back crying

by Hareshi Bhudia

Cockney Talk
One day
In my cat and mouse
I was in my tan and red
I got up.
The rag and bone was ringing
so I put on my almond rocks
and my dicky dirt
because my whistle and flute
was in the cleaners
I went down the apples and pears
I picks up the rag and bone
and I hears the joanna playing
next door
It was driving me mad
so I put on my daisy roots
and I goes down the frog and toad
to the bloke next door

151

so I gives him a tinkle
and I says, 'Keep the racket down'
I can't hear myself on the rag and bone
so I goes back to my cat and mouse
and the person was gone
so I went down the local
to get elephant's trunk.

by Tony Day

The class teacher, Jane Quigley, was doing a project on 'Second Homes'. She asked the children to go home and talk to their parents and grandparents about other places they had lived; think about places that they themselves had been to and she brought in a James Berry poem about 'His Island'. When they got to writing, I tried to get them to work on trying to remember exactly what mums and dads said or exactly what things they remembered from their visits.

Notice Hareshi takes off on his own. This is what I mean about children inventing their own forms. You never know how, why or when, but it happens. It always gives us a chance to explore new ways of writing.

Notice also, Terry and Tony's poems. In a class that was predominantly second generation emigrants, these were two cockney boys who didn't have 'second homes', as such. I always that in situations like that, it is vital that children like that are not left spare, it only stores up trouble for later.

Coming home on my own thinking
Coming Home on my own Thinking
Couldn't Wait to get home Thinking
Buzzing of the planes engines Thinking
Couldn't wait to meet me friends Thinking

I'll miss this cold country Thinking
Coming home Guyana Thinking
back to the nice warm weather Thinking.

by Brenda Dundas (13 plus)
Brenda just handed this to me in the library one day. I love it. How she invented the form, why she felt like writing it, why she handed it to me — I don't know the answers to any of these questions, I'm afraid.

Breakfast Time
What's happening in here?
I feel sleepy
I don't want to brush my teeth
I don't want my hair brushed
It's time for school, love
I love this bacon
My toast is burnt
Don't be rude
Don't open your mouth when you're eating
Tidy up your bedroom, you
I don't want to
Hold the baby
Be a good girl
We're going to the Natural History
Museum today
Mum, can you make us a packed lunch, please
Oh, I need spending money
I'll be late for work
Mama mama mama I want my breakfast mama
I lost my nail polish
Who's taken my lipstick?
Mum, the dog's nicked me sausages
Mum, I don't want to go school today, it's PE

A group poem on all the things that people are saying to you at breakfast time.

When Michael Rosen comes into my class
I say to him,
'You can play marbles with your eyes.
'And sometimes your eyes poke out
like they are on springs.
Your hair is like undone knitting.
Your nose is like a bad carrot.'

by Robert

No comment.

APPENDIX III
The Way We Speak to Each Other
(Summary Guidelines)

1. The bragging, boasting voice. 'You ought to have been there last night...' Exaggerating: 'On the back seat of the coach or bus...' With deflationary last line.

2. The voice of power and authority. 'And where do you think you're going?' Headmaster, doctors to patients, farmers to trespassers, police. Orders, commands, instructions, rules.

3. The guilty voice. 'What me?'

4. His/Her relationships. 'What's the matter?' 'Well what would you like to do?' Splitting up (a telephone conversation). First meeting. Encounters.,

5. The teasing, mocking voice. 'You look a right one you do!' 'What are you going red for?'

6. Street voices. Hanging around with nothing to do, during the summer holidays, calling, crying. Being called in for tea.

7. Sulky voice. 'You go and do that then! I don't mind.'

8. Trying to be more grown up than I actually am voice. Trying to get in to an X certificate film. Impressing a stranger. Voice put on at a disco. Talking with a vicar.

9. Looking up to somebody voice. 'Can I have your autograph, please?' Hero/heroine worship. 'I wished I looked like...'

10. Getting on with parents/adults voice. 'Oh Mum, please can I...' 'Why only me then?'

11. Telephone voices. Complaining, soothing, leaving a message with an Ansaphone service, arguing, having to say 'Thank You' after Christmas or a birthday etc.

12. The joking voice. 'Enjoy your trip!' 'You and whose army?'
13. Bus conversations.
14. Supermarket or corner shop conversations.
15. Interview conversations.

by David Jackson *
(author and teacher)

*David Jackson's "Destroying the Baby in Themselves: Why Did the Two Boys Kill James Bulger?" is available from Five Leaves.

Appendix IV
BIBLIOGRAPHY

Collections by individual poets, many of whose poems are very 'oral'.
Please note that some of these books are not in print but I have included them as they are still available in libraries and resource centres.

I Din do Nuttin
John Agard
Red Fox

Say It Again Granny
John Agard
Little Mammoth

Grandfather's Old Bruk-a-Down Car
John Agard
Red Fox

When I Dance
James Berry
Puffin

Playing a Dazzler
James Berry
Puffin

Duppy Jamboree
Valerie Bloom
Cambridge

Nearly Thirteen
Jan Dean
Blackie

Grow Your Own Poems
Peter Dixon
Macmillan Education

How to Handle Grownups
Jim and Duncan Eldridge
Hutchinson

More Ways to Handle Grownups
Jim and Duncan Eldridge
Hutchinson

What Grownups Say and What They Really Mean
Jim Eldridge
Hutchinson

Standing on the Sidelines
John Foster
Oxford

My Heart Soars
Chief Dan George
Hanock House, 19313 Zero Avenue, Surrey, BC V3S 5J9,
Canada

Spin a Soft Black Song
Nikki Giovanni
Sunburst , Farrar Strass and Giroux, USA

Vacation Time
Nikki Giovanni
William Morrow and Co., USA

Something On My Mind
Nikki Grimes
Dial, USA

The All-Nite Cafe
Philip Gross
Faber

Swings and Roundabouts
Mick Gowar
Collins Lions

15 Ways To Go To Bed
Kathy Henderson
Macdonald

Junk Mail
Michael Harrison
Oxford

Strange Goings-On
Diana Hendry
Viking

The Phantom Lollipop Lady
Adrian Henri
Magnet

Two's Company
Jackie Kay
Puffin

Three Has Gone
Jackie Kay
Puffin

Poems Selected for Young People
D.H. Lawrence
Macmillan

Birds, Beasts and The Third Way
D.H. Lawrence
Julia MacRae

Hey World, Here I Am
Jean Little
Kids Can Press, Toronto, Canada

All My Own Stuff
Adrian Mitchell
Simon and Schuster

Catching the Spider
John Mole
Blackie

Boo to a Goose
John Mole
Peterloo Poets

Picnic on the Moon
Brian Morse
Turton and Chambers

Knock Down Ginger
Brian Moses
Cambridge

Don't Look At Me in That Tone of Voice
Brian Moses
Macmillan

Plenty of Time
Brian Moses
Bodley Head

Midnight Forest
Judith Nicholls
Faber

Dragonsfire
Judith Nicholls
Faber

Come Into My Tropical Garden
Grace Nichols
Collins Lions

Taking My Pen For A Walk
Julie O'Callaghan
Orchard

Speaking for Ourselves
Hiawyn Oram
Mammoth

Girls Are Like Diamonds
Joan Poulson
Oxford

Quick Let's Get Out of Here
Michael Rosen
Puffin

The Hypnotiser
Michael Rosen
Scholastic

You Wait Till I'm Older Than You
Michael Rosen
Puffin

The Martians Have Taken My Brother
Rowena Somerville
Red Fox

Singing Down the Breadfruit
Pauline Stewart
Red Fox

The World is Beautiful
Rabrindanath Tagore
The Tagore Centre UK

Poems
Vivian Usherwood
Centerprise

If I Were In Charge of the World and Other Worries
Judith Viorst
Atheneum, USA

Mud Moon and Me
Zaro Weil
Orchard

Candy and Jazzz
Dave Ward
Oxford

Anthologies containing a good few poems written in 'oral' style

This Poem Doesn't Rhyme
ed. Gerard Benson
Puffin

He Said, She Said
ed. Anne Harvey
Puffin

Oral Poetry from Africa
eds. Jack Mapanje and Landeg White
Longman

'Ere We Go
ed. David Orme
Macmillan

Dear Future... A Time Capsule of Poems
ed. David Orme
Hodder

Toughie Toffee
ed. David Orme
Collins Lions

The Secret Lives of Teachers
ed. Brian Moses
Macmillan

Some 'wordy' books for children

Wicked Words
Terry Deary
André Deutsch Children's Books

Kids Book of Wisdom, Quotes from the African American Tradition
eds. Cheryl and Wade Hudson
Just Us Books, 356 Glenwood Avenue, East Orange, NJ 07017

The Silent Beetle Eats the Seeds, Proverbs from Far and Wide
ed. Axel Scheffler
Macmillan

The Cat's Elbow and Other Secret Languages
coll. Alvin Schwartz
Sunburst, Farrar, Straus and Giroux, USA

See also the poems of Allan Ahlberg, Charles Causley, Roger McGough, Colin MacNaughton, Gareth Owen, Brian Patten, Jack Prelutsky, Shel Silverstein, Kit Wright, Benjamin Zephaniah. All these poets use very clever rhyme and verse techniques, which young children find hard to use when writing about things that are what I've called 'authentic'.

Permissions

ALSO AVAILABLE FROM FIVE LEAVES

The Golem of Old Prague
by Michael Rosen and Brian Simons
These tales of the old Prague ghetto are mysteriously eerie and threatening, but the realism of the humour gives a reassuring earthiness. The atmospheric stories are complimented by new line drawings and wax prints by Brian Simons.

Michael Rosen is a broadcaster, writer and poet. He is the author of many best-selling books for children. Brian Simons (Boruch ben Yitzchak) is a teacher in North London.

The Golem of Old Prague is suitable for 11 year olds and upwards.

105 pages, 0 907123 96 1 (pbk), £5.99

"Adhering strictly to the unflinching candour of the folk tale... The Golem of Old Prague is a beautiful, and unfortunately, timely book." **Times Educational Supplement**

The Bend in the Road: Refugees Writing
(ed) by Jennifer Langer
The Bend in the Road is a collection of fiction, poetry and memories by refugee writers. The book covers all aspects of refugee life, including being in exile, memories of home, fleeing, women's experience, resistance. Most of the 50 or so writers have been published widely in their country of origin, including Miroslav Jancic (Bosnia), Sousa Jamba (Angola), Sherko Bekas (Kurdistan), Buland Al-Haidari (Iraq), Pius Ngandu Nkashama (Zaire) and Maxamed Ibraahim 'Hadraawi' (Somalia).

The Bend in the Road also outlines the literary tradition of the main countries "providing" refugees to Europe and sketches the recent history of those countries.

Jennifer Langer, herself the child of refugee parents, works with refugees in London.

208 pages, 0 907123 37 6 (pbk), £8.99

Destroying the Baby in Themselves: Why Did the Two Boys Kill James Bulger?
by David Jackson
"I would recommend it as essential reading for anyone working in the field of male violence prevention." **Achilles Heel**
48 pages, 0 907123 31 7 (pbk), £3.50

Haunting Time

by David Belbin

Haunting Time is a collection of eerie and ghostly tales.

From the all-night bookstore to the deserted library, from the funfair to those you meet on holiday, things — and people — are not quite what they seem.

David Belbin is the UK's best-selling crime writer for young adults. He is the author of *Shoot the Teacher, Final Cut, Love Lessons* and the *Beat* series.

Please write for details of class sets of *Haunting Time*. Teaching notes are aslo available from Five Leaves.

248 pages, 0 907123 62 7, £5.99, published October 1998.

Poems for the Beekeeper: An Anthology of Modern Poetry

(Ed) by Robert Gent

A selection of the most popular poets on the modern poetry circuit, many of the poems included have never been published before.

The 37 contributors include Danny Abse, Fleur Adcock, James Berry, Wendy Cope, Carol Ann Duffy, Helen Dunmore, U.A. Fanthorpe, Mick Imlah, Jenny Joseph, Jackie Kay, Liz Lochhead, Henry Normal... you get the picture?

138 pages, 0 907123 82 1 (pbk), £6.99

All Five Leaves' titles are available through booksellers. Please send a card to go on our mailing list.

Five Leaves Publications, PO Box 81, Nottingham NG5 4ER.